## Titles in the series

Celebrity Stalkers
Celebrity Court Cases
Crime Scene Investigation
Crystal Meth
Dangerous Dogs
Deadly Mission
Hurricane Katrina Survival Stories
Identity Theft
Inside the War in Afghanistan
Killer Flu
Most Wanted Terrorists
Plastic Surgery Case Studies
Plastic Surgery Gone Wrong
Road Rage
Terrorism: The Homeland Threat
Wrongfully Accused

**www.amazingstoriesbooks.com**

## LATE-BREAKING
# AMAZING STORIES™

# ALIEN ENCOUNTERS

**Strange events and
unexplained phenomena**

*by Rennay Craats*

PUBLISHED BY ALTITUDE PUBLISHING LTD.
1500 Railway Avenue, Canmore, Alberta T1W 1P6
www.amazingstoriesbooks.com
1-800-957-6888

In order to make this book as universal as possible, all currency
is shown in U.S. dollars.

| | |
|---|---|
| Publisher | Stephen Hutchings |
| Associate Publisher | Kara Turner |
| Canadian Editor | Frank MacKay |
| U.S. Editor | Julian S. Martin |

We acknowledge the financial support of the Government
of Canada through the Book Publishing Industry Development
Program (BPIDP) for our publishing activities.

ALTITUDE GREENTREE PROGRAM
Altitude Publishing will plant twice as many trees as were used
in the manufacturing of this product.

**Cataloging in Publication Data**
Craats, Rennay, 1973-
    Alien encounters / Rennay Craats.

(Late breaking amazing stories)
ISBN 1-55265-319-6 (American mass market edition)
ISBN 1-55439-521-6 (Canadian mass market edition)

    1. Unidentified flying objects--Sightings and encounters.
2. Human-alien encounters I. Title. II. Series.

| | | |
|---|---|---|
| TL789.C72 2006a | 001.9420973 | C2006-901210-5  (U.S.) |
| TL789.C72 2006 | 001.9420971 | C2006-901243-1 (Cdn) |

In Canada, Amazing Stories® is a registered trademark of Altitude Publishing
Canada Ltd. An application for the same trademark is pending in the U.S.

Printed and bound in Canada by Friesens
2  4  6  8  9  7  5  3  1

"…The public does not want another 20 years of UFO confusion. They want to know whether there really is something to this whole UFO business—and I can tell you definitely that they are not satisfied with the answers they have been getting."

*Dr. Allen Hynek at a 1968 symposium on UFOs*

# CONTENTS

Photographs . . . . . . . . . . . . . . 8
1 An Alien Abduction. . . . . . . . . . . 15
2 The UFO Phenomenon . . . . . . . . . . 26
3 A Case for Alien Encounters . . . . . . 69
4 The Scientific Search for Aliens . . . . . 116
5 The Future . . . . . . . . . . . . . . 139

A Timeline of Alien Encounters . . . . . 143
Amazing Facts and Figures. . . . . . . . 149
What Others Say . . . . . . . . . . . . 155

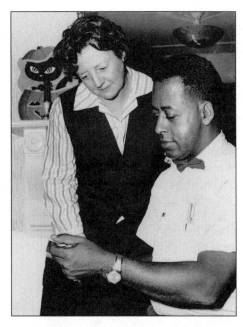

Barney and Betty Hill, photographed here in 1966,
claimed to have been abducted by aliens
in New Hampshire on September 19, 1961.
For more on their story, see page 81.

Charles Hickson, left, and Calvin Parker of Gautier,
Mississippi were fishing in the Pascagoula River on
October 11, 1973 when they claimed to have been
abducted by three aliens in an egg-shaped UFO. Their
ordeal lasted 20 minutes. The two men later passed
a lie detector test and have stuck by their story since.
Read about other alien abductions in Chapters 1 and 3.

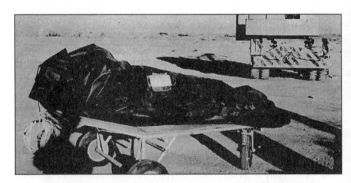

This photograph is taken from the U.S. Air Force's *The Roswell Report,* released June 1997, which discusses the UFO incident in Roswell, New Mexico in 1947. On balloon flights from Roswell, test dummies were placed in insulation bags to protect temperature-sensitive equipment. Some witnessess claims these "body bags" were used to recover alien victims from a UFO crash. The 231-page report was released on the eve of the 50th anniversary of the Roswell UFO incident. For more on the Roswell incident, see Chapter 3.

Jill Tarter, director of the Center for SETI Research, poses with a one-eighth scale model of the Allen Telescope Array, in Mt. View, California, in 2003. Three hundred and fifty of the full-size arrays will be deployed in Hat Creek, California by June 2008 to pursue the center's search for extraterrestrial intelligence. For more on the scientific search for aliens, see Chapter 4.

Chuck Clarke spends all his spare time at the
perimeter of Area 51 hoping to find out what
happens in this top secret military base near
Rachel, Nevada. For more information on
Area 51, see page 80.

Mike Esper of Howell Township, Michigan
looks for wheat stalks with burnt nodules in a crop
circle in his wheat field in 2003. He has no idea
how the crop circle got there. For more
information on crop circles, see page 104.

# CHAPTER 1

# An Alien Abduction

I t was a day like any other for 22-year-old Travis Walton and his six work friends. The young men, ranging in age from 17 to 28 years, were just finishing work thinning trees in the Apache-Sitgreaves National Forest near Snowflake, Arizona, early in the morning on November 5, 1975. While getting ready to leave the work site, they noticed a bright glow coming from the trees. As they drove away, they saw an object measuring about 20 feet (6 m) across and 10 feet (3 m) wide hovering above a clearing. Travis Walton got out of the truck and raced toward this strange object as his fellow crew members watched. When he was about six feet (1.8 m) from the disk-shaped entity before it began making odd noises. As Travis attempted to retreat, a bluish beam of light struck him hard, hurling him several feet backward.

Travis's friends were afraid and drove away quickly. A few minutes passed. When their fear subsided, they returned to the site to pick up their co-worker. He was nowhere to be found. They saw the disk-shaped object streak away. The six men searched the area for about 30 minutes, but Travis seemed to have disappeared without a trace. They had no choice but to leave the area and report this strange occurrence to the police.

The sheriff's officers returned to the area with the men and processed the scene. They found no evidence of Travis or of this odd encounter. The search for Travis Walton continued the next morning, again resulting in nothing.

The police began to question the men, figuring that perhaps they had murdered their coworker and invented an Unidentified Flying Object (UFO) abduction story to cover their tracks. Or perhaps Travis and his brother, Duane, had devised the ruse as a scheme to make money. There had to be a rational explanation—the thought of a UFO taking Travis away was just too unbelievable. The shaken co-workers were subjected to a polygraph test—five of the men passed the test. The results of the sixth test were inconclusive. The testimony of the men was enough to convince Sheriff Marlin Gillespie that there just may have been something to the UFO story after all.

Days of searching failed to turn up a clue as to Travis's whereabouts. On November 10, a late-evening telephone call was placed to the home of Grant Neff, Travis's brother-in-law. The caller sounded disoriented and weak. He claimed to be Travis Walton. He said he was at a gas station in Heber, Arizona, and Grant rushed off to get him. He and Duane picked up Travis, who was shaking from the cold and still wore the same clothes he had disappeared in five days earlier. While it seemed that the ordeal was over, it was really only beginning. Debate raged over what had really happened and where Travis Walton had been for five days.

Many police officers insisted that the entire scenario was a hoax. Others supported the claim that Travis and his friends had encountered a UFO. Two of Travis's supporters were Jim and Coral Lorenzen—directors of Aerial Phenomena Research Organization (APRO) in Tucson. They talked with Travis and offered to give him a polygraph test. The test's operator was skeptical, to say the least, and was openly hostile to Travis throughout the examination. After Travis failed the test, some people said it proved that he had fabricated the entire story, while others blamed the failed test on the stress of the abduction and the approach taken by the examiner. Another test taken a few months later, suggested that Travis's responses to questions about his experiences between November 5 and November 10 were truthful. His story always remained the same, with no deviations or elaborations.

Travis told police that once the beam of bright light hit him, he blacked out. He awoke in what he imagined to be a hospital room, without any recollection of how he got there. He had trouble breathing the air, which was heavy and humid, and his eyes could not focus well on his surroundings. Beside him, he discerned three humanoid figures with chalky-white skin. As his vision cleared, he began to focus on the "doctors" leaning over him. They were bald, with large eyes and small ears, noses, and mouths. They wore soft, orange overalls over their approximately five-foot frames. They silently stared at Travis with their bulging eyes. "The sudden horror of what I saw rocked me as I realized I was definitely not in a hospital," recalls Travis. "I was looking square into the face of a horrible creature … with huge, luminous brown eyes the size of quarters! I looked frantically around me. There were three of them! Hysteria overcame me instantly." He remembers panicking, jumping off the bed, and trying to push past these beings. He grabbed for anything to use as a weapon but found nothing he could use to defend himself. His three "visitors" left quickly through a door behind them, and Travis followed shortly after in a bid to escape.

Travis ran into a room that was empty except for a tall metal chair in the center. As Travis approached the chair, the room's lights began to dim, and then they brightened as he moved away from the chair. He looked around and noticed small lights shining on or through the walls and floor. It was as though he was enveloped in stars. Travis wasn't sure if he was witnessing an illusion or if the room had suddenly become transparent. He approached the chair and found that it housed some kind of controls—levers and screens and buttons. He pushed buttons and handled the levers in an attempt to find a way out. Then he thought that they might be flight controls, so he decided to leave them alone, lest he crash or throw the craft off course.

Travis continued to study the room and the control chair until he heard a noise behind him. He quickly turned to find someone standing on the threshold. It appeared to be a man, clad in a blue spacesuit and helmet. Travis began asking questions and demanding answers of this man, but rather than clarifying anything for him, he led Travis out of the room and down a hallway. As Travis entered a very small room, he saw an open door that let in cool, fresh air. When he went through the door, Travis found himself outside the initial craft, in a large room with a curved ceiling. The craft he had left was similar to the one he had seen in the woods; only it didn't emit light and was larger. This craft was about 60 feet (18 m) in diameter and about 16 feet (5 m) high.

Inside this new area were shiny, saucer-shaped craft—two or three from what Travis could determine—that measured about 40 feet (12 m) across. He didn't have much time to look as the "man" led Travis through another door and yet another door, each opening mysteriously, seemingly with no prompting. Travis and the man walked into a white room containing a table, a chair, and three other beings, dressed in the same blue spacesuits but minus helmets. Many ufologists refer to these beings as Nordics, but at the time, Travis had no idea who or what they were.

One woman and two men gathered around the table and looked at Travis. He was struck by how good-looking they were and how similar to one another they appeared. Despite Travis's pleas, no one answered his questions or addressed him at all. They led Travis to the table and helped him up onto it. The woman placed a device, which resembled an oxygen mask without tubes, over Travis's face. Within seconds, his world turned black.

Travis Walton awoke to the feeling of cold pavement, as he lay flat on the ground. As he scrambled to his feet, he saw a streak of light zip off into the night and a huge silver-hued disk floating about four feet (1.2 m) above the road not far from him. Then it, too, suddenly and silently blasted into the sky, rustling the trees as it exited the area. He ran on wobbly legs down the highway until he came to the gas station from which he called his brother-in-law. He realized that it was late in the evening, so Travis assumed he had been unconscious for a few hours. He was aware of only about 60 or 90 minutes passing while he was aboard the craft. His brother and brother-in-law told him he had, in fact, been gone for days, and the growth of his beard confirmed that. Travis was shocked but grateful to be home after such a terrifying ordeal.

His homecoming wasn't quiet or peaceful,

however. His case had attracted international attention and everyone wanted to know what had happened. Skeptics were quick to ridicule Travis and his alleged experience, eager to cry hoax. While many claims of UFO encounters or abductions are met with suspicion and cynicism, few cases have been attacked as a deliberate hoax with such vigor as was Travis Walton's.

There was great attention paid to the case right from the start and every detail about the Walton family was suddenly telling. Some felt that the family's interest in UFOs before the abduction and the fact that they had watched a television movie about another abduction, that of Barney and Betty Hill, a few weeks before the disappearance, pointed to fraud. Many people claimed the hoax was a play for money. After all, the *National Enquirer* paid Travis $5,000 for his exclusive story, and his subsequent books and movie all earned him money over the years. He also gave speeches about his experience aboard the spacecraft. However, Travis continued to work in mills to support his family—hardly the payoff skeptics had accused him of master-minding from the beginning.

On the other side of the debate, believers rallied to Travis's side. Some people, who were often more neutral in their stance on alien life, suggested a natural or psychological reason for what transpired that week in November. This theory suggested that an earthquake had brought about hallucinations. However, this didn't answer the question of how Travis, dressed in light clothing, could have survived in the cold mountainous area for five days.

Travis and his family and friends defended their stories for decades, and it was even suggested that one of the men on the work crew was offered $10,000 to reveal the "real" story of what happened in the Arizona forest. He wouldn't change the story, as he and the rest of the men insisted that their initial report about what they had seen was the truth. In an attempt to quiet the non-believers, some of those involved even agreed to retake a polygraph test nearly 20 years later to remove the hoax cloud that hovered over them. The participating witnesses and Travis himself passed the test, supporting the UFO story and challenging the idea of an elaborate scheme. The experts calculated that, given the results, the odds of a hoax by all participants was less than one-tenth of a percent, suggesting that something happened that night in the woods. In the end, there were more than a dozen polygraph tests administered to witnesses in this case; some of them controversial or contested. This by no means was the end of the story or the fascination with it. In 1993, Paramount Pictures released *Fire in the Sky*, a film loosely based on Travis Walton's account of what happened to him in Arizona. Travis also wrote four books about his UFO and alien encounter.

For years afterward, this case continued to intrigue people within UFO circles and beyond. It was one of the first incidents of UFO encounters that told the story of gray aliens taking a strong role in the abduction of a human being—a story that would become more common in later years. It was also rare in that seven people witnessed the same thing, with one of them actually taken on board a craft for a period of time. As well, the people involved were not close friends or family but rather forestry workers brought together by employment. They didn't stay in touch over the years and there didn't seem to be anything for these men to gain from lying about what they saw. The mystery continues and likely will for years to come.

This spectacular story of alien encounter and abduction stirs the imagination of Hollywood directors and average North Americans alike. It's easy to dismiss as bunk, but there is something about the story, the circumstances, that raises the question, "What if?" That could well be the reason people continue to talk about, write about, and ponder the Travis Walton UFO abduction story 30 years after it came to light.

# CHAPTER 2

# The UFO Phenomenon

There's no doubt that for years North Americans have been intrigued by UFOs and alien visitation. It's fascinating to think that we are not alone, that other beings from other planets in other solar systems are watching or even making contact with us. The unknown nature of alien encounters has frightened people as much as it has fascinated them. The powerful 1938 radio play *War of the Worlds*, presented as a news broadcast, terrified Americans so much that many packed their belongings and hit the road or hid in their cellars to protect themselves from invading Martians. In the years that followed, Hollywood produced countless movies and television shows that delved into the murky world of other beings on Earth. From the heartwarming *E.T.* to the menacing *Independence Day*; from the thought-provoking content of *Close Encounters of the Third Kind* and *The X-Files* to the comedic representations of *Mars Attacks* and *Men In Black*, these programs sate the public's curiosity about the rumors of life "out there" and what would happen if "out there" became "in here." This curiosity and interest has been with us for centuries, through legends and stories that may have paved the way for the beginning of the UFO era.

## History of UFO sightings

For centuries, people have reported strange lights in the sky, strange beings in strange craft.

Stories of UFOs have been passed down as legends in many cultures. Chinese tales tell of a land of "flying carts." Sanskrit texts depict gods in flying machines with fireless blazes emanating from them. Even the Bible speaks of a "chariot of fire" and Jacob's vision of angels climbing into heaven on a ladder, which has been interpreted by some as a UFO occurrence. Ezekiel, too, had a vision involving strong wind and a great cloud surrounded by bright light and flashing fire from which came four beings. The beings had human form, but each had four faces and four wings. Some UFO researchers and believers interpret this passage as a UFO event as well.

History has recorded other possible UFO sightings and encounters. During the reign of Pharaoh Thermoses III in 1500 BC, there were reports that he saw a "circle of fire" in the sky and numerous bright disks that "had no voice." Alexander the Great said that two flying objects bothered his army in 329 BC. Ninth century French cleric Ago-bard, Archbishop of Lyon, wrote of his people being harassed by "aerial sailors" traveling on ships in the clouds.

The historical record is littered by possible references to UFOs, from the 1561 sighting of disks maneuvering in the sky over Nuremberg, Germany, to the 1791 sighting by astronomer Edmond Halley of objects lighting up the sky.

Documented sightings of strange objects continued throughout the 1800s and early 1900s as well. Between November 1896 and April 1897, a few reports of unusual, bright objects in the sky above California snowballed into more and more sightings of bizarre flying machines streaking eastward across the United States.

In 1908, the Siberian landscape was shattered, as something huge and mysterious exploded in the sky with such force that it broke windows, caused a powerful blast of wind, and smashed trees into splinters. Later, scientists estimated that the blast was on par with that of a 20-megaton nuclear bomb. Many people believe this explosion was the result of a UFO accident.

## WHAT IS A UFO?

Astronomer J. Allen Hynek defines a UFO as follows:

"The reported perception of an object or light seen in the sky or upon the land the appearance, trajectory, and general dynamic and luminescent behavior of which do not suggest a logical, conventional explanation and which is not only mystifying to the original percipients but remains unidentified after close scrutiny of all available evidence by persons who are technically capable of making a common sense identification, if one is possible."

Source: *The UFO Experience: A Scientific Inquiry* (1972)

Between 1909 and 1913 another wave of sightings was experienced around the world, with witnesses reporting cigar-shaped objects emitting bright lights overhead. This wave-like nature of UFO movement and sightings was something that would be repeated in modern cases as well.

Whether these events were indeed UFO-related or were explainable aerial events may never be known. They do, though, give researchers pause when considering how long UFO and alien visitation may have been occurring on Earth.

While there may have been many other UFO and alien encounters before, most researchers mark the beginning of the UFO era at 1947. It was on June 24 of that year that pilot Kenneth Arnold was flying over Washington State when he saw nine crescent-shaped objects whizzing ahead of him at what he estimated to be more than 1000 miles (1600 km) per hour. This exceeded the speed that even the newest jets could achieve. Kenneth reported his sighting and told reporters that the objects moved in a way that reminded him of a rock or saucer skipping across the water. Despite the fact that the craft he saw were crescent-shaped, the headline in the newspaper splashed the phrase "flying saucer" across the page—thus coining a term that would endure for decades and introducing North America to the world of alien and UFO encounters.

In the five years that followed Kenneth Arnold's sighting, the floodgates were opened across the United States, and reports of sightings poured out. It also inspired the press, scientists, and comedians alike to discuss and debate the issue of UFOs and alien visitation on Earth. What were these creatures' intentions, where did they come from, and were they ultimately hostile? The line in the sand was drawn in very thick, dark ink. Those on one side of the debate insisted there was truth behind the sightings. Those on the other side refused to entertain the notion of alien beings, regardless of the circumstances. Even the air force was forced to take UFO sightings seriously while downplaying the possibility of alien encounters publicly. This was a difficult task, especially given that some of its aircrews had come forward with strange sightings of their own. Meanwhile, the general public indulged in the countless stories of sightings in order to fill in the blanks left by a noncommittal government. In response, the government attempted to explain away, debunk, or ridicule reports of UFOs in hopes of being rid of the topic for good. But as more people reported encounters, the public continued to believe the impossible: that unidentified spacecraft were visiting Earth.

While the debate raged intensely, an event in Roswell, New Mexico in 1947 made it burn white-hot. Reports of a glowing object turned to allegations that an alien craft had crashed and the occupants of this craft were found. Conflicting information, changed stories, and cries of a government cover-up abounded in the weeks after this event, leading people to consider that perhaps there was something to this story after all. Even the skeptics were confused. The military held a press conference but didn't allow photographers close enough to what it was calling the wreckage of a balloon. Then a second photo opportunity was arranged, but this time the debris was different from that which was presented earlier. The fascinating, and at the same time terrifying, possibilities of aliens on Earth mesmerized Americans and riveted them to these stories.

People reported UFO sightings and some even provided photographs as proof of what they experienced. William Rhodes had heard a noise outside his home and rushed out in time to snap two pictures of an object zooming away, lights flashing. These photographs were published in *The Arizona Republic* on July 9, 1947, and were the first to capture this phenomenon on film. This prompted visits from the FBI and an air force intelligence officer to record Rhodes's story. Later, the authorities asked William for his negatives for assessment, which he turned over.

The newly established Project Sign (which became Project Grudge the following year) was created to covertly collect and study data about sightings. Officers from this project also visited William early in 1948, but the amateur photographer never heard from the authorities again and his negatives were never returned to him.

While some officers reported that they thought the photographs were legitimate, the sighting was considered a "possible hoax" without offering a reason or explanation. As new sightings and encounters surfaced, these and other earlier stories faded from memory and, in many cases, were never revisited.

Although officially not investigating UFO reports, researchers from the air force studied the flood of sightings to see if they could find common explanations for them. After six months, they found 156 of the reports needed a more thorough examination. By the end of 1947, the commanding officer in charge sent a note to Washington stating, "The phenomenon reported is something real and not visionary or fictitious." The UFO "problem" was not going away. It warranted more attention and scrutiny.

This became a higher priority when the UFO phenomenon claimed its first life. On January 7, 1948, people in Kentucky witnessed a bizarre object streaking across the sky. It was huge—about 250 to 300 feet (76 to 90 m) across—and was traveling very quickly as it maneuvered overhead. Three Air National Guard F-51 Mustang fighter planes that were readying to land were called to investigate. The crew described an object that was "round, like a teardrop, and at times almost fluid." They also noted that it was "of tremendous size." Captain Thomas Mantell alerted the base that he was going to try to get in for a closer look as the UFO climbed to 20,000 feet (6100 m). A few hours later, Captain Mantell was found dead in the wreckage of his plane. The air force investigators determined that he had blacked out because he didn't have enough oxygen to fly at that altitude. The air force then stated that the mystery object was really just Venus shining—an assertion that was challenged by comparing Venus's position at the time compared to the fighter pilot's.

Suddenly, UFOs and alien encounters weren't as easy to laugh off as they had been in previous months. It was seen as a serious and frightening phenomenon, and it prompted the government to bring in reinforcements to study UFOs.

## A TOP SECRET CASE

On July 24, 1948, an Eastern Airlines DC-3 was flying from Houston, Texas to Atlanta, Georgia in the early hours of the morning. When Captain C. S. Chiles and copilot J. B. Whetted saw a red glowing object in the sky, they thought it was a military jet; but the light headed straight for them. Captain Chiles veered to the left to avoid an impact and passed the object by only about 100 feet (30 m). They watched as this wingless, cigar-shaped object raced past at about 700 miles (1130 km) per hour, climbed sharply into the clouds, and disappeared amid orange flames.

Minutes after this sighting, Robins Air Force Base in Macon, Georgia reported a bright light traveling very quickly overhead. A subsequent report arrived a few days later in which a pilot near the Virginia–North Carolina border saw what he described as a bright shooting star. This case marked the first time two reliable sources were able to describe the same UFO sighting.

Some people suggested that the object was little more than a meteor or perhaps the result of overtired, overly imaginative, pilots. But even members of Project Sign were not convinced. This top-secret case was buried and copies of the report were burned.

Noted astronomer Dr. Allen Hynek, a professor at Ohio State University, joined the project and as a skeptic with impressive credentials, he was just the man the air force needed to help them discredit UFO sightings. His stance was that witnesses were often unaware of environmental or astronomical explanations that could account for the strange objects and events they were seeing. In many cases, ball lightning flashing through the sky, sun pillars breaking through the clouds, and lens-shaped clouds called lenticular clouds that closely resemble UFOs were to blame for false reports. These naturally occurring phenomena had generated UFO reports around the world. As well, comets, and later, faraway satellites, could also mimic the appearance of an unexplainable flying object.

Dr. Hynek evaluated UFO cases for the air force for 20 years, and although a staunch UFO debunker in the beginning, Dr. Hynek came to realize that not every report could be explained away. He found himself insisting that some cases merited more investigation and should not be dismissed as a waste of investigators' time. Dr. Hynek founded the Center for UFO Studies

(CUFOS), where he and others could scientifically evaluate UFO and alien encounter reports.

## PROJECT BLUE BOOK

Between 1947 and 1969, the U.S. Air Force began actively investigating sightings as part of a program called Project Blue Book. During that time, the organization probed 12,618 UFO sightings and of those, 701 were deemed unidentified.

Throughout the 1950s, compelling stories of UFO sightings surfaced that were difficult to dispel. Many involved reputable, credible witnesses, including military officers and engineers. The level of experience these military personnel had regarding airborne objects made it less likely that they would mistake a plane or a balloon for unidentified craft. Even more reports were revealed years later, delayed by witnesses' fear of ridicule and retribution from the government and society as a whole. Cases were still debated, but people were listening more attentively to reports of UFO sightings. However, people wanted proof—something indisputable—that UFOs and alien visitation were a reality.

In 1950, Americans took a step closer to this when Oregon farmer Paul Trent snapped two clear photographs of what he claimed was a hovering alien spacecraft. These pictures were a rarity in that the government investigators could not label them a hoax—but neither would they affirm that they depicted an authentic alien craft.

Decades later, these photographs were studied using computer programs and imaging. This evaluation determined that hidden supporting wires were not suspending the object in the photographs, as skeptics at the time had insisted. Color contouring techniques also allowed investigators to determine specifics about the contents of the photographs. It was found that the image was that of a three-dimensional shape with a flat bottom located about 0.6 miles (1 km) away from the photographer and measuring between 65 feet and 100 feet (20–30 m) across. The photographs passed this computer scrutiny with flying colors and researcher

William Spaulding supported Paul Trent's assertion that he had indeed captured a genuine
UFO sighting on film.

The next few decades saw many cases that
were difficult to refute, confirm, and classify.
While creating a logistical nightmare for the U.S.
government, they were embraced by UFO and
alien believers as authentic examples of visitation from another civilization.

Canadian authorities also created a UFO
study in the early 1950s under the Department of
Transport. Wilbert B. Smith, a radio engineer who
had already been investigating Earth's magnetic
field, headed this small and short-lived program.
The study hoped to explain "flying saucers" as an
extension of these magnetic principles. Project
Magnet was responsible for collecting and ana-
lyzing data, as well as using scientific methods to
determine if a report was "real."

In 1952, Smith concluded that UFOs used
magnetic principles and appeared to be the
work of other civilizations. The following year,

he deduced that many UFO reports involved alien vehicles created with technology that was clearly much more advanced than our own. To study the phenomenon, Project Magnet established a "flying saucer sighting station" outside Ottawa, Ontario in 1953, which was equipped with technology to detect alien spacecraft: a gamma-ray counter, a magnetometer, a radio receiver, and a recording gravimeter.

On August 8, 1954, these instruments picked up and recorded an unusual disturbance, but thick fog prevented researchers from seeing anything. Only a few days later, the government discontinued Project Magnet, but allowed Smith to carry on with his studies on his own time. He continued to study UFO activity in Canada until his death in 1962.

During this time, various dedicated scientists and academics began studying UFOs and alien visitation. Such professionals as Dr. Hynek, researcher and physicist James McDonald, University of California at Berkeley engineering professor James Harder, and engineer Robert M. Baker spoke out at a symposium in 1968, demanding that the topic of UFOs and alien encounters be taken seriously by the scientific community and the government. They argued that this topic was being unfairly judged and then dismissed. "On the basis of the data and the ordinary rules of evidence, as would be applied in civil or criminal courts, the physical reality of UFOs has been proved beyond a reasonable doubt," said Harder. There were others in attendance who did not agree, ridiculing the UFO phenomenon and its believers.

As always, there were two sides to the issue, each equally vehement in its beliefs. And mere months after the symposium, the Condon Committee finally released its report on the UFO phenomenon. The nearly 1,500-page document published by the University of Colorado UFO Project, analyzed UFO sightings and reports for scientific validity and was intended as the last word on the topic. The last word, according to

Condon, was that alien UFOs were not real and did not deserve any further time or resources.

But this last word was followed by many other words uttered by angry critics. They argued that the summary and the recommendations sections were all that most people reviewed; each was written by Condon himself, based not, they contended, on the cases contained in the report, but rather on his own beliefs. They pointed out that he did not mention that nearly one-third of the cases analyzed remained "unidentified."

In the end, the Condon Report gave the government and UFO skeptics the green light to dismiss UFOs as bunk and justified the cancellation of Project Blue Book. Paradoxically, the report also gave UFO believers room to contend that the report represented biased analyses or perhaps an even further cover-up of the phenomenon. Despite the protest, it became clear that the government wanted to wash its hands of the entire controversy.

## A new phase in alien encounters

Beginning in the late 1950s and early 1960s, the UFO phenomenon developed beyond people seeing strange lights in the distance or finding unexplainable evidence of a craft's visit to Earth. People now began claiming that they were encountering the occupants of these craft face to face, sometimes seeing them from a distance and, in some instances, being abducted by them. These experiences, classified as "close encounters," brought a new dimension to the issue of aliens on Earth.

The first recorded abduction report was that of 23-year-old Antonio Villas Boas in Brazil in October 1957. He reported being taken from his farm by large-headed beings in tight-fitting gray suits. While on board, he was examined, had blood drawn, and even claimed he had a sexual encounter with a female entity before being returned to his farm. The young man claimed that he subsequently suffered from numerous medical ailments as a result of his encounter. He complained of nausea, headaches, burning eyes, lesions, and strange painful nodules that appeared on his body for several weeks afterward. After interrogation and examination by military personnel, Boas's story was generally accepted as an "actual occurrence." As reports of abductions became more frequent, they introduced a profile of alien beings that were allegedly studying humankind, one person at a time.

## Alien types

No one has yet been able to photograph alien beings during all of these reported encounters, but many people have sketched these creatures. Throughout the years, many commonalities have emerged in the various descriptions of these beings.

The most common of the reported alien races are referred to as "the Grays." These creatures are usually about 3.5 feet (1.1 m) tall and have whitish-gray skin. Their heads are large and bald, and host enormous dark eyes that often appear to wrap around their heads. They have a narrow jaw, no discernible nose but have tiny nostril holes, and thin, lipless mouths. Grays have slender torsos, arms, and legs. Each hand has three fingers capped by claws rather than fingernails. In some instances, witnesses have modified this general description. Some of these variations of grays include different skin colors and body types—some are as tall as seven feet or have darker skin, while others may have four fingers or have hands with suction cups on the ends of the fingers, instead of claws. Grays are usually dressed in robes, tight-fitting jumpsuits, or nothing at all. Some alien believers place the number of types of Grays at 12, which is something they say isn't unusual if you consider the number of different races there are on Earth.

Nordics are another reported alien type that closely resembles human beings. These beings are so named because of their Scandinavian appearance: attractive, pleasant, and kind, with a tall stature, blue eyes, and blond hair that is

## HYNEK'S CLASSIFICATION

In Dr. Hynek's book *The UFO Experience: A Scientific Inquiry*, he developed a classification system to define different sighting types and three different levels of contact between humans and UFOs or alien beings. The fourth and fifth kinds were added years after Hynek's book was published to accommodate the changed climate of alien encounters.

### Distant Sightings
**Nocturnal Light**
- Lights observed at night

**Daylight Disk**
- An unidentified object (of varying shape) observed during the day

**Radar Visual**
- An object noted on radar that is also verified by a visual observation.

### Close Encounter of the First Kind
- When a UFO comes close to an observer (or overhead) but doesn't physically affect him or the environment.

### Close Encounter of the Second Kind
- When a UFO is witnessed close-up and some evidence of the UFO's presence is left behind, for example electromagnetic radiation or an aura. This electromagnetic effect has been known to disable or slow car engines or affect a vehicle's electrical system.

## HYNEK'S CLASSIFICATION (CONTINUED)

**Close Encounter of the Third Kind**
- Encounters involving humanoid beings making contact with observers during the visitation.

**Close Encounter of the Fourth Kind**
- Covers all forms of abductions, including examinations and investigations by aliens, before the abductees are returned more or less unharmed.

**Close Encounter of the Fifth Kind**
- The rarest encounter type, this involves humans being taken for flights on UFOs.

often worn long. Encounters with Nordic beings were the first to be reported in the 1950s and 1960s but have waned as the primary alien species reported on Earth. Some alien enthusiasts surmise that this human appearance is really just a screen memory or illusion called upon to prevent abductees from panicking about being taken by an alien being.

Another alien type has been dubbed the Praying Mantis. These creatures have long, narrow faces with elongated upward-slanting eyes. Praying Mantis aliens greatly resemble the insect for which they are named, down to the long, thin limbs, crooked arms with a sharp bend at the joint, and a crouched stance.

Some people have also reported seeing scaly aliens that have been dubbed Reptilians or Reptoids. The fine scales, yellowish-green eyes, and snout-like face give them the appearance of a lizard. These tall, powerful creatures are thought to be very advanced technologically and quite hostile.

Unlike the Hollywood characters played by Will Smith and Tommy Lee Jones, Men in Black are actually another reported type of alien. Completely hairless and dressed in black suits and ties against white shirts, Men in Black (MIB) are threatening creatures that often visit UFO witnesses or researchers. People who have been contacted by MIB often report that the purpose for these robotic human-like creatures' visits is to discourage witnesses from talking about their experiences or seeking additional information about UFOs and aliens. They also report that MIB speak using language peppered with outdated gangster jargon from B-movies. After a short 10-minute visit, the MIB leave, apparently weakened by appearing before the witnesses. MIB have been reported since the 1940s, but many researchers today argue that Men in Black are in fact either an illusion, created after an encounter as a way for frightened people to cope with what they saw, or are just plain hoaxes.

## Characteristics of UFOs

What makes a UFO a UFO? This seems to be a difficult question to answer. Witnesses have described UFOs in a variety of ways and have attributed a variety of characteristics to them. Many UFOs are reported as saucer- or disk-shaped, triangular, or cigar-shaped. There are some reports detailing UFOs that resemble helmets or boomerangs as well. Alien craft are often symmetrical but some have flattened bottoms with domed tops.

Despite their different shapes, there are a

number of characteristics common to many reported UFOs. While a general rule is difficult to establish, given the diversity of UFO reports, most of these vehicles seem to fall within basic parameters. These craft are usually between 15 and 100 feet (4.6–30.5 m) across but most commonly measure less than 30 feet (9 m) in diameter. Since these vehicles appear to weigh between 30 and 60 tons, it's surprising that they produce little more than a faint humming noise when they fly. Most reports tell of fast-moving lights—some bluish-white, others red or green—that can range in brightness.

UFOs are also reported to release electro-magnetic energy, which would account for reports of burns on the skin and irritated eyes. In some cases, UFOs are believed to emit radiation that could lead to radiation sickness with close contact. The energy associated with UFOs is also thought to interfere with, and in some cases disable, nearby automobiles' electrical systems. Many reports mention that observers' vehicles stalled or that their lights malfunctioned for the duration of the sighting.

The UFO, as described, is a marvel in flight. These vehicles appear devoid of visible or audible propulsion systems yet are seemingly able to maneuver skillfully at great speeds. UFO speeds have been estimated between 10,000 and 12,000 miles (16,000–19,300 km) per hour. The craft are capable of changing direction, speed, and altitude very quickly and simultaneously. Many UFO sightings have reported these spacecraft hovering, spinning while hovering, or even resting on edge while hovering. Some craft are even said to wobble slightly from side to side as they slowly approach Earth.

As they near the ground, many UFOs are believed to leave behind swirled or burned grass at the landing sites, or to affect the roots of plants or even change chlorophyll in the foliage. In addition, close contact with UFOs has led many witnesses to report a strange and unpleasant odor emanating from UFOs that some say reminds them of ozone or formaldehyde. Some observers also claim that the UFOs they encountered had some type of force field protecting them, which deflected rocks hurled at them or even bullets.

The consistency with which observers worldwide have described the appearance and behavior of UFOs has strengthened the argument that sightings are real and that alien visitation warrants further evaluation.

## Ebb and flow of alien encounters

With the dawn of the 1970s, it seemed that while investigation methods were becoming more thorough and scientific, interest in the phenomenon waned. The number of reported sightings dropped. It was unclear whether fewer people were experiencing extraterrestrial visitation or those who did feared the scorn and suspicion that would surely be heaped upon them if they came forward. Skeptics continued to bash believers, arguing that UFO and alien sightings were explainable: some resulted from natural occurrences, while others were the figment of observers' imaginations.

However, in 1973, the dip in reports suddenly reversed and became a torrent, as sightings flooded in from every part of the United States, involving every kind of encounter. The air force was again faced with having to investigate these claims, some of which were quickly classified and then buried. One such case involved an army helicopter crew who, while flying over Ohio, noted a red light following their aircraft. They could not call air traffic control to report the light as it rapidly approached them at about 700 miles (1120 km) per hour and their radios suddenly malfunctioned. Captain Lawrence Coyne jerked the controls and dipped under the cigar-shaped object, which then stopped suddenly and hovered above them. The strange craft then quickly sped toward the horizon and disappeared. The crew lost control of the helicopter, which ascended at about 1000 feet (300 m) per minute for approximately 100 seconds before it regained control. During this time, the compass spun rapidly and needed to be replaced after the trip. Captain Coyne and his crew reported the incident and while he never wavered from what he claimed he had seen, Coyne added the disclaimer that he didn't believe in UFOs. Given the crew's training and sophistication, it was difficult for the air force to ridicule or explain away this experience.

Similar sightings continued across the country until the wave slowed in 1974. Some of the civilian and military reports of UFO sightings during this period were covered by the media but most were not revealed until the advent of the Freedom of Information Act. With it, UFO researchers dove into provocative accounts of UFO sightings and alien encounters, as well as reported abductions from decades past.

Another surge of sightings occurred in the United States from 1982 to 1983, during which time thousands of people reported seeing unusual objects in the sky. The decade was marked

## SAGAN'S PARADOX

In the early 1970s, Carl Sagan, noted astronomer, argued that it was scientifically unlikely that the UFO reports were related to extraterrestrial visitation. He said that for UFOs to visit Earth with such regularity, there had to be something unique about this planet to make it worth the effort. This, he said, goes "exactly against the idea that there are lots of civilizations around. If there are lots of them around, then the development of our sort of civilization must be pretty common. And if we're not pretty common, then there aren't going to be many civilizations advanced enough to send visitors." Sagan believed that given the billions of stars in the universe, it is quite probable that there is not only intelligent life, but also highly civilized life, out there. But he did not believe that aliens were traveling to Earth in UFOs.

by UFO sightings, and the Center for UFO Studies alone fielded between 800 and 1200 reports each year.

Major UFO waves were also reported in South America, Great Britain, and Belgium throughout the 1980s. It would appear that sighting and encounter numbers remained strong entering the nineties and the phenomenon showed no signs of going away. From the brightly lit roman candle-like object observed descending and then exploding over McMinnville, Tennessee in 1994, to a mass of sightings of cigar-shaped objects and "fireballs" inhabiting the skies of the southwestern United States in 1996, Americans' eyes seemed fixed to the skies.

One case in particular attracted a great deal of attention. The 1997 "Phoenix Lights" case involved thousands of witnesses—law enforcement officers, pilots, scientists, architects, doctors, and other reliable citizens—observing an enormous triangular object passing or hovering overhead across Nevada and Arizona. This object, which was adorned with lights, flew silently and very quickly; some witnesses guessed it was traveling at supersonic speeds. Air traffic control personnel and commercial airline pilots reported seeing this object, but it did not register on radar.

A report from Luke Air Force Base west of Phoenix stated that an F-15C fighter was launched to investigate the phenomenon, but as the pilot intercepted the huge object, his radar system suddenly malfunctioned and the object's lights faded, causing it to disappear from the pilot's sight. Senior officials from the base denied receiving reports about such an event, but telephone records indicated differently. Investigation into this bizarre and widespread sighting continued for years, but much of what was reported remains unexplained and controversial.

Sightings of strange objects in the sky and encounters with alien beings rang in the 21st century and have continued steadily since. In 2001, a Michigan mother of two reported being abducted from beside her sleeping husband—paralyzed and terrified of the creatures that had taken her. In 2003, a person in Florida reported being taken and examined aboard an alien spacecraft before being returned home. Countless other UFO sightings and alien encounters and abductions are being reported every day.

In December 2005, the National UFO

Reporting Center logged 249 reports, and almost 500 were logged in October of that year. With access to the Freedom of Information Act and calls for full disclosure, UFO and alien researchers are hoping to access information to support their position and to fill any holes left by cover-ups and misinformation.

## Opening up

In the 1970s, many individuals and organizations employed the Freedom of Information Act to force the United States government to finally open its files regarding the UFO phenomenon. Slowly, such agencies as the FBI, the National Security Agency (NSA), and the CIA, as well as the U.S. military, began releasing their documentation. Some, such as the FBI and NSA, have made their UFO documentation available over the Internet, leaving retrieval and deciphering up to the individuals requesting it. While not proving that secret government projects were in operation, the breadth of this documentation did show that these organizations had a long-term interest in UFO and alien reports.

The FBI became active in UFO investigation in the 1940s in conjunction with the air force, after Kenneth Arnold's reported sighting in 1947. The military then called upon the FBI to investigate reports of downed disks, even though it considered them a hoax. J. Edgar Hoover refused to waste his manpower on something thought to be a ruse, so he withdrew his FBI investigators from the UFO realm altogether.

The NSA, which monitors global communications that could affect U.S. security, had many more UFO documents than the FBI. Despite the order to turn over information regarding UFOs, much of NSA's material was riddled with deletions and blacked-over text relating to places, witnesses' names, and other details. This has made further investigation into these cases virtually impossible.

The CIA worked closely with the U.S. Air Force throughout the 1940s and 1950s, as the number of UFO sightings soared. It was investigating the sightings more as potential national security threats than alien invasions. A study group, part of the Office of Scientific Intelligence (OSI) and the Office of Current Intelligence (OCI), was established to investigate the UFO situation in the United States. While it concluded that most reports were easily explained, the acting chief of the OSI, Edward Tauss, recommended that they continue to quietly monitor the issue to prevent public alarm—Tauss did not want to suggest that the agency was confirming that UFOs existed.

Responsibility for UFO investigation was then moved to OSI's Physics and Electronics Division, where investigators studied UFOs as they related to national security threats. The study group, along with air force officials, came together with their findings and conclusions. The air force contended that only 10 percent of reports were worthy of a deeper look, but it did not believe the evidence contained within these sight-

ings related to secret Soviet weapons or alien beings. Instead, investigators claimed the reports
were a result of misinterpretation of explainable
objects or natural phenomenon. The CIA and air
force agreed to keep the agency's involvement
and interest in UFOs classified. This conceal-
ment led to later accusations of a CIA conspiracy
and cover-up of known alien visitation.

A number of other programs and pan-
els studying the UFO threat reached the same
conclusion as the previous groups had: UFOs
presented neither a national security threat nor
evidence of extraterrestrial visitation. It was,
however, concluded that the public's fixation on
UFOs and alien encounters could disrupt national order. By debunking reports and dissemi-
nating information about the lack of evidence
proving the existence of UFOs, these findings
could avert potential hysteria. Reports and details about group activities were stamped "classified" and the CIA began to gradually step back
from UFO investigations.

Government interest in UFOs was motivated in large part by a concern with enemy activities. At the height of the Cold War, agencies were investigating whether UFOs could have been weapons or craft developed by the Soviets or even a ploy to overload U.S. air-warning systems, allowing for a possible nuclear strike. They considered that UFOs could be used to create panic across the United States, thus weakening it. The United States, Canada, and Great Britain were working together to develop an unconventional saucer-like aircraft and the CIA was concerned that perhaps the former Soviet Union was doing the same. These factors kept at least some of the CIA's attention on the UFO phenomenon.

By the mid-1950s, the U.S. government was testing high-technology projects, including the U-2 aircraft. It could fly higher than any other commercial airplane and was silver, reflected the sun's rays, and could appear fiery from the ground. When the military began testing these aircraft, the number of UFO sightings skyrocketed. The government could compare flight schedules with reported sightings to explain away about half of them at the time. Other high-profile UFO or alien sightings have been explained by claiming that what was seen were instances of top-secret testing of military technology.

Whatever the reasons for these sightings and encounters, people wanted to know the truth. However, public pressure to know the details of government involvement fell on deaf ears. The CIA refused to release classified documents. The need to protect confidential military operations, along with a desire to keep the CIA's involvement in UFO investigations secret, led to mounting criticism and accusations even as the agency pulled resources away from UFO study in the late 1960s and 1970s. Throughout the remainder of the century, the CIA and other groups watched the UFO issue, but not in an organized, significant way.

All the while, claims that the government and its agencies have withheld important information about UFOs and alien visitation on Earth continue to be voiced. Government officials have maintained that UFOs do not threaten national security or indicate the existence of extraterrestrial life, yet released documentation regarding its research on the topic is often blacked out or incomplete—quite inconsistent with its original claims. It has become clear to many ufologists that the truth in many of these cases may never be known.

Whether the clandestine nature of the governments' treatment of the UFO phenomenon was to protect military initiatives or to calm a jittery country, is not clear. Despite controversy, scientific ambiguity, and possible misperceptions of events, a large number of people across North America maintain that alien and UFO encounters are a reality.

# CHAPTER 3

# A Case for Alien Encounters

In the realm of alien encounters, there are many different ways that otherworldly beings make contact. In some cases, people witness unusual lights. In others, they see unexplainable craft in the sky. Some report experiencing face-to-face contact with aliens that led to abductions and examination. There are myriad accounts of alien encounters over the past half-century.

## Controversy in New Mexico

In late-June 1947, reports of disk-like objects flashing through the sky throughout the country ran in the newspapers. Then around July 5, a New Mexican rancher named William Brazel, whom friends called Mac, found some strange material strewn about his Corona ranch. With all of the stories about flying disks, Mac reported the debris to George Wilcox, the sheriff in nearby Roswell. The report then found its way to the local army base. There, base commander Colonel William Blanchard entrusted his head intelligence officer, Major Jesse Marcel, and the head of the Roswell Army Counterintelligence Corp., Sheridan Cavitt, with the investigation. The two officers and Mac collected some of the debris from the ranch and brought it to the base for examination. They also ensured the area was secured, keeping all non-military personnel away from the scene.

That afternoon, Glenn Dennis was working a shift at the Ballard Funeral Home when he

received a strange phone call from Roswell Army
Air Field. The man on the other end was inquir-
ing about four-foot-long (1.2 m), hermetically
sealed caskets. Glenn had one such casket and
asked if there had been an accident. The officer
replied that it was for future reference and hung
up. He called back later to ask how one might
handle bodies that had been exposed to desert
conditions—again claiming that it was research
for the future.

Glenn, who also provided ambulance ser-
vice, later dropped an airman off at the hospital,
where he saw strange debris in the back of another
ambulance. A nurse told Glenn to leave before he
landed himself in trouble. But before he had the
chance, he was threatened and ordered to leave.
A base nurse told Glenn later that she had been
part of a preliminary autopsy of strange, small
bodies with large heads, large eyes, concave noses, and thin mouths. She was soon transferred to
Europe before she could relay any further information about the mysterious events.

The day after the collection of debris, the air force released a statement to the press detailing a "flying disk" recovered on a ranch. The debris from this disk had been transported for more thorough research. The media clamored for more information about the mysterious crash. What exactly was this disk, and how did the air force account for the strange sightings in the area in the weeks before?

About an hour later, the military began altering the account of what happened at Roswell. They said that, rather than a disk, the rancher had found a crashed weather balloon as well as its radar target. The unusual debris Major Marcel had left earlier in Brigadier General Roger Ramey's office was replaced with the remains of a weather balloon, which was offered up to photographers to dispel rumors of unidentified craft on American soil. Ramey insisted that there was nothing particularly noteworthy about this discovery after all, and that once the military brought in a weather officer to confirm that the debris was in fact the remains of a weather balloon, the story could be put to rest.

Not everyone was convinced by this new story. Major Marcel and Brigadier General Thomas Dubose later stated that it was all a government cover-up—one Dubose claimed he was personally ordered to launch. Mac Brazel was also brought into the cover-up, affirming the weather balloon story with his descriptions of the debris on his ranch. But he affirmed that there was something unusual about this event, stating at the end of the interview: "I am sure that what I found was not any weather observation balloon, but if I find anything else besides a bomb they are going to have a hard time getting me to say anything about it." Mac's reluctance to become involved may be attributed to his alleged detainment for several days by the military, while the debris was removed from his ranch.

Many people believed that the crash object was indeed an alien spacecraft and that the military was hiding the truth from the public.

Some people suggested that there had been a collision between two alien craft, and that one was destroyed and was found on Mac Brazel's property. The other, supporters say, landed a distance away. The alien life forms allegedly on board—alive, dying, or dead—were recovered for examination as well.

Other supporters believe a spacecraft was hit by lightning and crashed on Mac's ranch. If this was the case, the government was then, and is now, aware that aliens have been to Earth and has been studying alien technologies found at the crash sites. Since the 1940s, the government has vehemently denied the alien version of events at Roswell and continues to maintain that the debris was that of a downed weather balloon.

But many facts work against the balloon story. People who had seen the debris stated that it had properties the likes of which they had never seen before. Some pieces looked like foil, but the material was impossible to crease,

## SOME OTHER EXPLANATIONS FOR ROSWELL

**Project Mogul Balloon:** The crashed craft was really a top-secret balloon designed to detect Russian A-bomb tests. The debris itemized from the Roswell crash was similar to that expected of the early Mogul balloons: about two dozen rubber weather balloons, attached radar targets, and wood kites covered with foil or paper. These arrays could also span up to 600 feet (180 m), explaining the large debris field reported. The balloons were cutting-edge, so likely would have seemed out of this world to civilians encountering them.

**Nuclear Accident:** Some people contend that Roswell was the site of a nuclear weapons accident. The "flying disk" and the cover story were a distraction from the fact that a nuclear weapon had been lost. However, the United States did not have nuclear weapons assembled at the time.

**The "Horrible Secret":** In 2005, researcher Nick Redfern published his opinion that the Roswell crash was of an experimental spy craft manned by a captured Japanese flight crew. The experiment failed and crashed, and the government was forced to cover it up to avoid the "horrible truth" from surfacing: that the military had illegally detained and used Japanese POWs for these experiments. No documents back this theory of the crash or indicate that any program like this existed.

## FOREIGN TECHNOLOGY

In 1997, Colonel Philip J. Corso, the former head of the Pentagon's Foreign Technology in Army Research and Development, released a book called *The Day After Roswell*. In it, he confirmed that the military indeed acquired alien technologies from reverse-engineering recovered spacecraft from Roswell. He claims that technology originating from that 1947 crash has led to laser technology, fiber optics, microchip technology, and night vision equipment, along with countless other classified advancements.

wrinkle, bend, or dent. Other pieces looked like lightweight wood, but they too, could not be destroyed, cut, or burned. The debris was described as being adorned with symbols akin to hieroglyphics and was said to appear *otherworldly*—and many people believed it was exactly that. As well, claims of bodies taken from the scene fueled the public's imagination, but the official statement was that the craft was clearly too light to support passengers. The mystery of what landed near Roswell in 1947 subsided but has never dissipated entirely.

## Alien autopsy

Decades after the Roswell crash, interest in the possible recovery of aliens re-ignited, as researchers dove back into the stories. By the 1960s, witnesses to the event—both civilian and military—were speaking about what they knew and what they had heard during the Roswell investigations. Some, including air force Brigadier General Arthur Exon, claimed to have heard about additional UFO crashes and recoveries, and about studies that were conducted on the craft and on onboard aliens. Other people, including Dubose, claimed that the cover-up at Roswell was ordered from the highest power in the country—the White House—and that it was classified with a rating even higher than top secret.

In 1995, the furor surrounding Roswell and the alien landing was again awakened when a film surfaced purporting to show an alien autopsy. Ten reels of 16 mm black-and-white film—allegedly shot by an ex-military cameraman named Jack Barnett and presented to British film producer Ray Santilli—showed a six-fingered, six-toed being with a big head and big eyes, but otherwise quite human-like, being medically examined. The film is grainy with poor lighting, poor focus, and shaky camera work. The frames show surgeons in hazardous materials suits bent over the body of this supposed alien.

The debate over its authenticity raged in and out of UFO circles. Pieces of the film were analyzed by experts to determine when the footage was shot, but there were claims that the film was from a different program altogether. The film has never undergone extensive testing. Kodak did verify that the code on the film showed it was manufactured in 1927, 1947, or 1967, as the company repeated the pattern every 20 years. Many people claimed that special effects professionals could easily have created the so-called alien for the autopsy film. If the government wanted the autopsy filmed, critics argue, it would stand to reason that they would get a more professional camera operator, or at the very least, provide a tripod to improve the film quality. As well, the doctors did not follow common surgical and scientific procedures during the examination, all of which led skeptics to point to a hoax.

At the same time, believers argue that the secret, sensitive nature of the incident would encourage the authorities to use the people and equipment that were available. Requests for professionals or better equipment would leave evidence and a paper trail. However, no documentation for "Jack Barnett" has surfaced, making some people doubt Santilli's story. That said, many ufologists say there is no evidence proving it is a hoax and they remain open to the idea that the footage may truly be an autopsy of an alien taken from the Roswell crash.

Whether a hoax, an authentic autopsy, or a disinformation tactic by the government to discredit the notion of aliens at Roswell, the footage only fuels the controversy of the New Mexico crash of 1947. Even after nearly 60 years, there

## AREA 51

Also known as Groom Lake, Paradise Ranch, The Farm, and Watertown, "Area 51" is a clandestine facility just north of Las Vegas for the development and testing of military aircraft projects. This remote area was the site of bombing practice during World War II and U-2 spy plane testing in the mid-1950s. Today, Area 51 continues to operate as a testing ground for new aircraft before they are made public. The government does not openly acknowledge the area or its purpose and it remains off-limits to civilians, as well as standard military personnel. Regardless, a staff of more than 1800 people work at the high-security facility.

Many ufologists associate this 6-by-10 mile (10-by-16 km) tract of land both with UFO landings/encounters and with a government-wide cover-up. They claim that alien spacecraft have been stored, examined, and even recreated at Area 51 and that recovered aliens themselves have been studied there. Some people even claim that a large underground facility exists at nearby Groom Lake or Papoose Lake for the study of alien technology and individuals. In the late-1990s, the United States Air Force admitted the existence of a base alongside the dried-up, makeshift runway at Groom Lake. A statement said that aircraft testing during the Cold War could account for many of the UFO sightings that had occurred.

is no definite proof for either side. That doesn't matter to the town of Roswell. It has become a tourist Mecca, hosting UFO and alien festivals, conferences, and a museum.

## The grandparents of ufology

Barney Hill refused to believe that what he and his wife, Betty, saw in the sky that September night in 1961 was a UFO. A skeptic at heart, Barney insisted that the bright light moving in the sky was a plane or a satellite. Betty, on the other hand, was convinced the unusual object was nothing as common as that.

On September 19, the Hills were returning home to Portsmouth, New Hampshire, from a vacation in Canada when they viewed an odd light around 10:15 p.m. They stopped a few times to let their dog out and kept an eye on this strange light, which seemed to be following them. It also got bigger and Barney watched it streak to the west and then return to where the Hills could see it, coming closer each time it returned. Soon, the flat object was only about 100 feet (30 m) away from their car.

During a stop at Indian Head, Barney watched the object through his binoculars and saw different colored lights and rows of windows along the craft. Barney left the car and approached the mysterious craft. After seeing beings looking down at him from rows of windows, Barney panicked and raced back to the car. The Hills quickly sped off, trailed by a beeping sound they couldn't identify. A short while later, they heard the beeping again, followed by silence. The rest of their journey was uneventful.

The next morning, Barney noticed some damage to his car for which he could not account. Blotches of paint had been stripped away to bare metal. Betty's sister had read that magnetism was often associated with UFO encounters, so Barney passed a compass over these points. The needle jerked violently over the bare patches: the spots were magnetized. As well, Barney suffered from a pain in his back and had unexplainable scuff marks on his shoes—the kind that would result from a person being dragged along the ground. The Hills were confused by all of this and Betty, against Barney's wishes, decided to contact nearby Pease Air Force Base to report what had happened to them. The couple was not told anything at the time, but later, a radar report surfaced of a UFO sighting in that area at the same time as the Hills reported their experience.

Barney Hill wanted to forget the whole matter and get on with his life. However, Betty was engrossed in the UFO encounter. She researched UFO sightings and alien encounters at the library, reading with zeal such resources as The Flying Saucer Conspiracy by Major Donald Kehoe. She wrote to Kehoe, telling him about those strange events in September. She began having horrifying dreams about 10 days after they encountered the UFO. These vivid nightmares—which featured the couple stopping at a roadblock and then entering a large spacecraft inhabited by beings with cat-like eyes—continued for about five days and then faded.

Meanwhile, Major Kehoe was interested in the Hills's story and passed Betty's letter to Walter Webb, a scientific adviser for the National Investigations Committee on Aerial Phenomenon (NICAP). Webb drove to Portsmouth in October to visit with Barney and Betty, listening intently for hours while the two described the events during their return from Canada. The report Webb compiled compelled others to travel to New Hampshire to talk with the Hills the following month. One of these men asked a pivotal question: Why did it take the Hills so long to get home? Given the mileage and the time of night, Barney and Betty should have arrived home about two hours sooner than they did. Neither had any idea where that lost time went. It did, however, prompt the couple to take the advice of friends and consult with a psychiatrist.

Barney and Betty delayed their therapy, trying to continue with their lives. But the health problems Barney suffered before the encounter—ulcers and hypertension—became worse and his doctor suggested the cause might be emotional. Barney, and Betty soon after, began regression therapy with Dr. Benjamin Simon to finally uncover what happened during those missing two hours.

In separate sessions, Betty and Barney told the same story of a UFO hovering near the road and those inside forcing the Hills aboard. During some sessions, other staff members had to help Dr. Simon restrain Barney as he relived the traumatic abduction. Both Barney and his wife were medically examined by these alien beings and had samples taken before they were finally released. Before Betty left, however, she asked the aliens from where they hailed. Under hypnosis, Betty related to the doctor the aliens' origin, even reproducing a detailed sketch of a star system called Zeta Reticuli that she had been shown.

Dr. Simon believed the Hills had experienced a trauma that night, but he wasn't convinced that

## ZETA RETICULI

Zeta Reticuli is a star system in the constellation Reticulum that is about 39 light years from Earth. It can be seen only from south of the tropics and can be viewed without a telescope when the skies are very dark. Many ufologists believe that Zeta Reticuli is home to an alien civilization that visits Earth and even abducts humans.

aliens had abducted the pair. His diagnosis was that Betty had created the abduction scenario in her dreams in order to fill in the missing block of time. Barney, having heard about the vivid dreams, unconsciously adopted her explanation to account for the missing time.

The Hills were disturbed by the outcome of their therapy: they were no further ahead than when they started. They still weren't exactly sure what had happened and were discouraged by Dr. Simon's doubt in the veracity of their story. With more counseling from other doctors, the Hills seemed to find peace with what had happened, accepting that they had been abducted.

While they may have become more comfortable with the experience, they certainly weren't looking for publicity, but in October 1965, they got it anyway. After Barney and Betty spoke with NICAP, a reporter received part of the story and approached the Hills for the rest. The couple refused to comment, so the reporter ran what he had, in an article in the *Boston Globe*. European newspapers picked up the Hills's story and the New Hampshirites began receiving early-morning phone calls looking for comments. They were nervous about this publicity.

Betty worked as a social worker at the state welfare agency and Barney worked for the post office and was the governor of New Hampshire's Civil Rights Commission. Both were apprehensive about the ridicule and disbelief that was bound to follow their incredible abduction account. They feared they would lose their jobs because of it. Their employers were supportive, but pressure mounted for Barney and Betty to go public themselves.

On November 8, 1965, Barney agreed to be filmed for television at a small Unitarian church in Dover. The interview drew a packed crowd, including John G. Fuller, an author who would later write *Interrupted Journey* about the Hills's sensational case. Interest in the case also led to the production of a television movie called *The UFO Incident*, starring James Earl Jones and Estelle Parsons.

What made this case so remarkable? This was the first abduction story to be made public. It took years for the Hills to reach a conclusion about what had happened to them that September night. They offered consistent accounts and descriptions, and the air force base backed up their sighting. Further lending credibility to the case, the Hills weren't looking for fame or fortune with their alien encounter claim—they were simply looking for answers. Both of them held down good jobs and had nothing to gain by going public with their experience. The Hills case has endured as a pivotal example of alien encounter and abduction, even though critics were quick to find other explanations for what

Barney and Betty remembered experiencing. One thing skeptics could not explain away, however, was Betty's sketch of the star system Zeta Reticuli. She was able to create a detailed drawing of this system six years before astronomers had even discovered it.

## In aliens' backyards

NASA is dedicated to finding and exploring new life in space. According to many individuals involved in various Apollo missions in the 1960s and 1970s, life has been found.

While stationed at Edwards Air Force Base, California in 1951, astronaut Major Gordon Cooper and his crew saw a disk-shaped object hovering nearby. They happened to be filming the new landing facility, so they kept the camera rolling, capturing the bizarre event. The film was sent to Washington, classified, and has never been released.

Then in 1963, Cooper orbited Earth 22 times during NASA's last single-manned

mission. During this mission, he reported seeing a glowing object approaching him. This object was confirmed by radar at the tracking station at Muchea near Perth, Australia. These two
events made Major Cooper a believer, and he
spoke openly about his beliefs and experiences.
He said, "For many years, I have lived with a secret, in a secrecy imposed on all specialists in
astronautics. I can now reveal that every day, in
the U.S.A., our radar instruments capture objects of form and composition unknown to us.
And there are thousands of witness reports and
a quantity of documents to prove this, but nobody wants to make them public."

*Apollo 14* astronaut Dr. Edgar Mitchell was
the sixth man to walk on the moon. He claimed
that he heard first-hand accounts from military
and professional people, regarding close encounters while in space, but they are unable to
publicize these experiences. He acknowledges
the government's efforts to cover up information about UFOs and alien beings and hopes

that one day the truth about alien visits will be forthcoming.

North Americans were glued to their televisions in July 1969 when Neil Armstrong stepped onto the moon, but many people think there was more going on than one giant leap. There are unconfirmed reports that during this mission, Neil Armstrong and Buzz Aldrin encountered alien beings who instructed them to leave the moon permanently. Many people believe that there were alien craft hovering near the landing sites, as well as evidence that artificial structures had been built on the moon.

Maurice Chatelain, NASA scientist, inventor, and designer of the Apollo communications and data processing systems, supported the belief that astronauts encountered other spacecraft. "It seems that all the Apollo and Gemini flights were followed, both at a distance and sometimes also quite closely, by space vehicles of extraterrestrial origin—flying saucers or UFOs, if you want to call them by that name. Every time it occurred, the astronauts informed Mission Control, who then ordered absolute silence."

Few astronauts are willing or able to come forward with any alien experiences, due to strict restrictions imposed by NASA and the government. However, the rumors about such sightings and experiences persist today.

## Air force sightings

The area around Bentwaters Air Force Base just east of Ipswich and Lakenheath RAF Station northeast of Cambridge in Great Britain has been the setting for some unusual sightings over the years. On August 13, 1956, at around 9:30 p.m., a U.S. Air Force airman stationed at RAF Bentwaters noticed an unidentified object flashing on his radar screen. Given the time it took to progress across the screen, Airman Second Class John Vaccare estimated its speed at between 4800 and 6000 miles (7,500–9,500 km) per hour. Within a few minutes, there was a group of three objects flying in a triangular formation followed by up to 15 more objects appearing around the base. They then came together to form one large object much larger than the B-36 aircraft—the biggest operational bomber of its time, measuring 230 feet (70 m) across.

At 10 p.m., the radar picked up an object traveling over 12,000 miles (19,000 km) per hour. Less than an hour later, the base radar screens showed an unidentified object traveling west at 2000 to 4000 miles (3200–6400 km) per hour, and Bentwaters control tower reported a bright light over the field that remained in the area for about an hour, alternately disappearing and then reappearing. At the same time, a pilot flying over the military base reported, "A bright light streaked under my aircraft, traveling east to west at terrific speed." The actual speed of the object is not certain, but it was agreed that this high speed was not compatible with any conventional aircraft of the time.

Strange sightings continued and around 11:30 p.m., the RAF sent a deHavilland Venom jet interceptor to investigate. The pilot saw a bright light, but when he neared it, it disappeared. Nearby Lakenheath RAF Station directed the pilot to different coordinates to converge with the blip on the screen. The pilot located the light, but it suddenly maneuvered around the interceptor and repositioned itself on the aircraft's tail. The pilot tried to lose the object but couldn't, so an additional interceptor was sent to the location. The first pilot stated, "He—or it—got behind me and I did everything I could to get behind him and I couldn't. It's the damndest thing I've ever seen." Sightings similar to these were reported until about 3:30 a.m.

What makes these 1956 sightings unusual—and more credible—is the documentation of the more than five-hour event and the different ways in which the objects were detected. Radar images were supported by people on the ground, who saw lights moving in unexplainable patterns, and by pilots, who viewed the events from above. There was also no known astrological or aeronautical explanation for the appearance of the objects; meteors don't move erratically as these objects did. Nor can they stop and change direction quickly and at such high speeds.

The air force's Condon Report, which addressed several unidentified object sightings, stated that this case remained unexplained. Although it did not flatly concede alien presence at Bentwaters and Lakenheath, the report did state, "The probability that at least one genuine UFO was involved appears to be fairly high." The Condon Report concluded: "In summary, this is the most puzzling and unusual case in the radar-visual files. The apparent rational, intelligent behavior of the UFO suggests a mechanical device of unknown origin as the most probable explanation of this sighting. However, in view of the inevitable fallibility of witnesses, more conventional explanations of this report cannot be entirely ruled out."

In 1980, air force personnel at Bentwaters again experienced bizarre sightings. On

December 26, radar picked up an unidentified object over Rendlesham Forest, which is surrounded by several military bases. USAF Sergeant John Burroughs recalled "a bank of lights, differently colored lights, that threw off an image like a craft." A security officer with Sergeant Burroughs remembered a triangular object emitting various lights and housing something inside—the "shapes did not look human," he said. The men also tried to investigate the forested area, but their vehicle wouldn't run and the lights wouldn't turn on around the sighting location, as if the power were being drained.

Security police commander Sergeant Adrian Bustinza claimed to see a circular object that was tapered at the edges, and that bulged in the middle, hovering in a clearing. There were also triangular shapes burned into the ground at spots where tripod legs would be needed to support a craft, and radiation was found to be emanating from these points on the ground. By 4 a.m., the original craft had either split into five smaller objects or had been joined by them before streaking through the sky and disappearing.

Little was heard about this strange sighting until a Freedom of Information request was filed two years later. The released report confirmed a strange glowing triangular object in the forest. It was about 6.6 to 9.8 feet (2–3 m) across and about 6.6 feet (2 m) high. This bright object was observed hovering, standing on legs, and then flying through the trees where it disappeared. An hour later, the object was seen again for a brief time before disappearing. In the early hours of the morning, the report stated, the object became five separate objects before disappearing. The report also detailed Beta/Gamma radiation readings in the depressions found on the forest floor.

While this information is compelling and provocative, more conclusive proof may exist. The encounter was allegedly filmed, and the tape was delivered to the USAF European head-quarters in West Germany for evaluation. The air force hasn't acknowledged the film, nor has the public seen the footage. But there is little dispute that something extraordinary occurred at Bentwaters, which the military personnel involved could not explain.

## Abduction in Manhattan

The abduction story Linda Napolitano, a 41-year-old mother of two, has the makings of a blockbuster novel: the Big Apple, mysterious events occurring in the wee hours of the morning, government agents, kidnappings, and controversy. But in this case, ufologists and a handful of witnesses insist this is no case of fiction.

At 3 a.m. on November 30, 1989, Napolitano, who was given the alias Linda Cortile to protect her identity, recalled feeling a presence with her in her room. She experienced paralysis as she lay in bed. She said she was then taken from her bed, floated out her closed apartment window 12 stories above the ground, and sucked into an alien spacecraft hovering nearby; blue-white lights aglow. Then the oval-shaped craft zipped away without so much as a whisper, with Linda on board. Linda said alien beings then examined and interrogated her before releasing her from the examination room. She suddenly found herself back in her own bed.

Linda (Cortile) Napolitano's case is unique in many ways. Hers involved a sighting and abduction in the middle of a major city, rather than the secluded rural areas commonly associated with the phenomenon. In most cases, abductees have no recollection of being taken and transported to an alien craft. However, Linda remembered the kidnapping vividly. Using hypnotic regression, Linda was able to relive the terrifying experience of being ripped from her bedroom and levitated high above Manhattan. Also, witnesses of an abduction, especially people with no relation or connection to the victim, are extremely rare. Witnesses to this case came forward to UFO investigator Budd Hopkins, whom Linda had subsequently contacted about her experiences. As Hopkins studied the case, letters from people claiming to have witnessed Linda's abduction arrived in his mail. The details given in the letters corroborated Linda's description of that morning. Adding extra credibility was the fact that two of the witnesses claimed to be government agents on bodyguard detail for a senior United Nations statesman and said they were taking the gentleman to a heliport when they saw the UFO. Hopkins believed the VIP to be Javier Perez de Cuellar, former UN secretary general. Hopkins attempted to convince de Cuellar to publicly support Linda's claims of being abducted, but he refused—he was referred to as the "Third Man" in Hopkins' 1996 book about the case, *Witnessed: The True Story of the Brooklyn Bridge UFO Abductions.*

More witnesses slowly came forward, painting a picture similar to that already sketched out by Linda and the two bodyguards. One woman, a retired telephone operator who had been returning from a late-night party on the night in question, told Hopkins a year and a half after the abduction that she saw a bright object near an apartment building as she drove over the Brooklyn Bridge. Her car stopped and the power went out, but the light from the craft was so bright she had to shield her eyes. She saw four figures float out of the apartment window and into a craft. Confused and afraid, this woman vowed never to return to New York City. Other witnesses thought that they had been watching a scene from a science fiction movie.

The most surprising part of the story may well be the subsequent behavior of the two alleged agents who witnessed Linda's abduction. They had contacted Hopkins in February 1991 to give him their stories and to make sure Linda was all right after her ordeal. The two men, known only as Richard and Dan, visited Linda and shared their emotional reaction to what they saw. They followed and watched her, trying to determine if she was legitimate or a fraud. A few months later, Linda claimed that Richard and Dan accosted her on the street, forced her into their vehicle, and grilled her for hours about the aliens and the abduction. She said the two men kidnapped her again in October. They demanded answers about the event and insisted she admit that it was a hoax, hoping to relieve their own anguish about the event. Linda asserted that she saw the men twice more that year, but was able to evade them. Through letters to Hopkins, each of the men stated that they were suffering mental torment from witnessing the abduction: Richard had taken a leave of absence and Dan was committed to an institution in order to get psychiatric help in dealing with the trauma.

While compelling evidence was gathered over six years of investigation, Hopkins never met face to face with these witnesses, thus had no direct evidence that they existed at all. As well, skeptics question why more witnesses didn't come forward in a bustling city like New York, even at 3 a.m. No one from Linda's apartment complex or the security guard stationed there saw or heard anything unusual that night. As well, the heliport on the east side was closed between 7 p.m. and 7 a.m., discrediting the alleged agents' story of where they were going when the abduction occurred. Linda's refusal to press charges against "Richard" and "Dan" for kidnapping, reinforced the skeptics' dismissal of her abduction claims.

The story of Linda Napolitano's alien abduction and the odd events following it began to attract significant attention. It was also revealed that Linda was no stranger to alien encounters; she had been abducted several times over the course of her life. She even claimed to have had a coiled implant inserted in her nostril during one abduction, and said the aliens examined it during the November morning kidnapping. After each encounter, she was returned to where the alien beings had found her, leaving her with a foggy recollection of events and a heart full of fear. Napolitano continues to tell her story of alien abduction without deviation today, despite attacks by skeptics. It remains one of the highest-profile UFO abduction cases.

## Mysterious crop designs

Mysterious and beautiful, crop circles have intrigued people around the world for centuries. They have also caused great debate as to how they are created and by whom. Some people claim that pranksters are responsible for the elaborate designs flattened into fields of anything from wheat to ice. In some cases, this is true. There have been cases of small groups of people entering fields under the cover of darkness and manufacturing a crop circle with basic tools.

But that does not account for all of the reported crop circles around the world. Much study has been conducted to find out the "truth" behind these enigmatic formations. Some studies suggest that crop circles result from cymatics—the visual representation of vibrations. This suggests that sound frequencies are at the root of the flattened crops, with higher frequencies producing more complex shapes. What might cause these frequencies, however, has not been determined.

Others believe that beams, such as microwaves from a satellite, are causing the designs to appear—intense microwave energy can cause stems to wilt in much the same way as crops in these circles are bent. Still others hypothesize that crop circles are formed by tornadoes or freak winds, by ball lightning, or plasma vortices.

As well, the natural existence of fungal circles is often pointed to when discussing crop circles. These figures are created when mycelium—which is the vegetative part of a fungus—spreads to make a circle. In some

## PLASMA VORTICES

A vortex can form high above the ground in a large cloud and then swirl to the ground in much the same way as a tornado. This can also be accompanied by light in the form of lightning. Plasma vortices were among the earliest theories to explain crop circles.

areas of the world, mushrooms or puffball fungi form circles and have been referred to in folklore as "pixie circles" or "fairy rings" created by elfin beings. Though commonplace, these circles exist on a much smaller scale than do the crop circles that ufologists study.

One scientist has put a great deal of time and resources into studying crop circles. After 17 years of study, Dr. Colin Andrews believes that about 80 percent of crop circles are man-made, and the rest may be the result of magnetism. A shift in the magnetic field can create a current that essentially electrocutes crops, causing them to flatten to the ground. These creations are often more simplistic than the elaborate designs favored by hoaxers. While this may be a valid explanation, the possible cause of this sudden and strange magnetic shift remains a mystery.

In other cases, the phenomenon is harder to explain away. Many witnesses report seeing bright balls of light and hearing strange noises emanating from where crop circles have materialized, and at times these crop circles appear to have been created in mere minutes. The phenomenon is similar to supposed UFO landing sites, where the grass beneath the craft is flattened in a swirling pattern while remaining undamaged.

In cases of some crop circles as well, the stalks of the crop field are bent rather than broken, which is impossible to achieve using the planks and rollers pranksters use. Crop circle researchers contend that an intense pulse of heat softens these stems, allowing them to bend at 90 degrees and then harden again without being harmed. As well, crop circles can contain up to five layers of weaving—each flowing opposite to the next—something inconsistent with hoaxes or pranks. Researchers suggest that heat, high-pressure infrared, and electromagnetic frequencies might all be applied to sites to create crop circles. Cell phones and batteries are known to malfunction around these areas and frequencies associated with crop circles have been known to interfere with helicopters and aircraft.

The shape of crop circles is also indicative of their makers. While pranksters using planks create perfectly rounded circles, other examples are slightly elliptical. As well, these mysterious circles incorporate obscure theories of geometry. Over the years, the patterns of crop circles have become more complicated and they have grown to span larger areas—some measuring 200,000 square feet (18,580 m$^2$).

Many people believe that these fascinating designs are evidence of something beyond us, of an encounter with an otherworldly presence. Whether these enigmas are created by UFOs as a message or by human artists seeking a new canvas, they continue to draw people with their mystery.

## Summer camp sightings

On August 7, 1969, the calm of Lake Champlain at the Buff Ledge summer camp near Burlington, Vermont, was broken when two teenagers noticed a strange sight. Two counselors, 16-year-old Michael Lapp and 19-year-old Janet Cornell, were enjoying some quiet time while most of the campers attended a swim meet away from the camp. As the two sat on the dock watching the sunset, they saw a bright light in the sky. Michael thought it might have been a planet—perhaps Venus—but the light grew brighter and moved closer to them. Then several lights broke away from the bright light and began dancing over the lake. A couple of the lights faded, but one disappeared into the lake, resurfaced, and then an object flew toward Michael and Janet.

They spotted two beings within the craft as it hovered over them. Michael screamed and put his arms around Janet to protect her. He remembered feeling like he was floating, and then the next thing the two knew, the campers were returning from the meet. The light, now in the distance, flickered occasionally before disappearing altogether. Time had passed, but neither counselor was sure of how much or what had happened during that period. In fact, Janet remembered little more than seeing odd lights over the lake that day.

Janet and Michael never discussed the experience or what it meant. After a decade of horrible dreams and reading about others who had experiences mirroring his own, Michael reached out to the Center for UFO Studies for help. Walter Webb, an investigator and lecturer on the subject, spoke with Michael to determine what had happened.

Under regression hypnosis, the now-26-year-old provided details about being abducted by alien beings that afternoon at the lake. He recalled being brought onto a spacecraft via a beam of light. There, he saw Janet on a table, being examined by small creatures. He described them as having "large eyes, mouths without lips, no ears, and two small openings for a nose." These aliens, who had webbed fingers and clammy hands, also medically examined Michael. They told him their goal was to recreate life, similar to that found on Earth, in another part of the universe. Then the teenagers were returned to the docks, with little memory of what had transpired.

Although Michael and Janet didn't stay in touch after their time at the camp, Webb was able to contact her. Using hypnosis with her as well, Webb heard a story of abduction from Janet that was strikingly similar to Michael's account, even though she hadn't heard his story. She spoke of being cold on a table and having something pinching her neck and pulling her hair.

Although 10 years after the fact, Webb investigated the story to confirm it as best he could. He found other campers who had seen bright lights over the lake and two other camp employees who claimed they had a similar experience at the lake. The stories inspired Walter Webb to write his 1994 book, *Encounter at Buff Ledge: A UFO Case History.*

---

### HITCHING A RIDE

In some cases, belief in UFOs can contribute to disturbed behavior. In March 1997, the largest American mass suicide took place in Rancho Santa Fe, California. Thirty-nine members of a religious cult called Heaven's Gate were moved to kill themselves with a lethal mixture of phenobarbital and vodka. The cult members believed that the comet Hale-Bopp, which was approaching Earth, was cloaking a UFO that would take them to a higher existence. By shedding their bodily confinements, the cult members believed their souls would board the spacecraft and be taken to another planet. While this is not a case of alien encounter, it shows the power of the belief in UFOs.

## Alien encounter pioneer

George Adamski was the first person in the world to publicly come forward with his claims of contact with UFOs and aliens. As proof, he provided photographs of spacecraft he said were taken with his telescope and even wrote books about meeting and traveling the cosmos with alien beings. His 1953 book, *Flying Saucers Have Landed*, was a best seller and his second, *Inside the Flying Saucers*, described what he experienced on board these spacecraft. Adamski said he watched as residents of the moon, "strolled down sidewalks." In his third book, *Flying Saucer Farewell* in 1961, he wrote about seeing "billions of fireflies ... flickering everywhere" during a trip to the moon aboard a Venusian spaceship. It would take eight years before some of Adamski's claims got some validation. U.S. astronaut John Glenn reported seeing similar "fireflies" during his space flight.

In all, Adamski reported more than 200 sightings around Mount Palomar where he lived, the first of which dated back to 1946. One of his best-known accounts of contact happened in November 1952, when he and some friends were in the Mojave Desert, California. He said he witnessed a large object in the sky and he knew a ship was seeking him out. He approached it and was met by a scout ship that landed close by. He and a figure from the ship—human-like with long, blond hair and with tanned skin,

by George's description—communicated using hand signals and mental telepathy. George
claimed the being, named Orthon, was from Venus and spoke to him about the perils of nuclear
weapons and the spiritual dangers of technology to humankind. He also claimed to have encountered beings from Mars and Saturn, even
joining them on flights in space. UFO believers
supported Adamski, and he enjoyed international recognition and attention. He presented
lectures around the world to civilians, military
personnel, and royalty.

While some evidence existed for Adamski's
frequent alien encounters, scientific discovery
began to fly in the face of many of his claims.
Once it was discovered that Venus and other
planets could not sustain life, his credibility
was shattered. Images from the moon without
the city he said was there were also costly to
George's reputation. He continued to dispute
findings that went against his claims, and after
announcing that he was traveling to Saturn for a

conference, even his supporters turned on him. At the time of his death in 1965, most UFO enthusiasts and former admirers had discredited many of his claims, yet studies continue on his UFO photographs and film footage to this day.

# CHAPTER 4

# The Scientific Search for Aliens

There are many different groups and individuals who have sounded off on both sides of the alien encounter debate. Some are avid believers looking to bring more credibility to the existence of extraterrestrials on Earth, while others are skeptics looking for and demanding irrefutable proof of such existence before taking any claims seriously. Many substantial organizations are spending top dollar to attract scientists to study the idea of life in space. Many of these institutions employ the world's best scientists, supporting their quest for proof of extraterrestrial life. To do so, incredible resources are made available to create the best technology to answer the question: "Are we alone?"

## Searching for life

There are various organizations and groups focused on scanning the skies for some sign of life. In the study of alien life, SETI weighs in heavily on the debate. SETI stands for Search for Extraterrestrial Intelligence. The SETI Institute is a not-for-profit organization established in 1984 to conduct scientific research, as well as to educate the public about life in space. Its mission is to "explore, understand and explain the origin, nature and prevalence of life in the universe." An army of more than 100 educators, scientists, and support staff study in two separate centers: The Center for SETI Research and the Center for the Study of Life in the Universe (LITU). While LITU researchers focus on learning about how life began, survived, and evolved by watching for life in deep space, the Center for SETI Research searches for signs of life by attempting to detect its technology. Detecting signals from this technology may lead to discovering advanced civilizations elsewhere in the galaxy.

The search for extraterrestrial intelligence began in earnest after physicists Giuseppe Cocconi and Philip Morrison released a paper in 1959 that stated that microwave frequencies ranging between 1 and 10 GHz would be the best to use for interstellar communications. These low frequencies make it easier to send and receive signals, and lower frequencies also allow for shifts that occur as the source of the signal moves with the orbiting of planets. A frequency of 1.420 GHz was ideal, the physicists suggested, as it is the frequency sent out by neutral hydrogen, so it is often referred to as the "water-hole" frequency by SETI researchers.

The quest for knowledge, however, is not restricted to trained scientists. Budgets are limited, as there is currently limited private funding and no government resources for SETI research. SETI@home is an experimental undertaking that has linked computers via the Internet since 1999 to search for extraterrestrial intelligence. Anyone can become involved by visiting *www.setiathome.ssl.berkeley.edu,* to download a free program from the space sciences laboratory at the University of California, Berkeley. The computer program downloads and analyzes data from the Arecibo radio telescope in Puerto Rico and sends it automatically upon logging onto the Internet. The large radio telescopes, such as Arecibo, detect narrow-

## USING SETI@HOME

The SETI@home computer program is set up to complete four tests. It searches for spikes in power spectra, for rises and falls in transmission power, for three consecutive power spikes, and for pulses that may indicate narrow-bandwidth transmission. These tests aim to determine if and where intelligent life might exist in space.

bandwidth signals from space—which do not occur naturally—in an effort to pinpoint intelligent life "out there." If detected, this would confirm the existence of extraterrestrial technology. There are more than five million people participating in the SETI@home project in more than 100 countries around the world.

There are also plans to begin collecting data from the Parkes Observatory in Australia to analyze signals from the southern hemisphere.

While this extensive study has not yet provided conclusive indicators of life in space, it has suggested some areas worthy of additional analysis.

The University of California, Berkeley, launched another SETI project called "Search for Extraterrestrial Radio Emissions from Nearby Developed Intelligent Populations," or SERENDIP. This project analyzes radio telescope observations that are already being conducted by astronomers from the site. Initially, when the program began in 1979, a 100-channel analog radio spectrometer that spanned 100 kHz of bandwidth was used, but recent observations have taken advantage of more capable, sophisticated instruments that provide significantly more coverage. The most recent spectrometer, operating since 1999, offers a 168-million channel apparatus covering 100 MHz of bandwidth. These instruments are being used with many telescopes, including the NRAO 295-foot (90 m) telescope at Greenbank, West Virginia, and the Arecibo 1000-foot (305 m) telescope.

While most SETI scientists are focused on radio frequencies, some embrace the idea of communication via powerful lasers at optical wavelengths. This notion was first introduced in 1961 and since then the notion has evolved. Harvard University's Paul Horowitz, along with researchers from the SETI Institute, has begun studies into optical SETI using telescopes and photon pulse detection systems. High energy lasers and enormous focus mirrors, it is surmised, would appear thousands of times brighter than the sun to a remote civilization living along the beam's path. The light pulses could be programmed to move to different targets quickly, hitting all sun-like stars inside 100 light-years. It also could incorporate a detection system that would pick up another civilization's attempt to contact us using lasers.

There are currently several experiments into optical SETI underway, including Horowitz's team using Harvard's 5-foot (155 cm) optical telescope and a laser detector. This instrument is being used to survey stars and the optical SETI experiment is "piggybacking" that research. A joint initiative between Horowitz's Harvard-Smithsonian group and Princeton University will see another detector system mounted on Princeton's 3-foot (91 cm) telescope, and the two telescopes will be able to track the same locations simultaneously to reduce errors from detector noise. Additional projects, including one at University of California, Berkeley, and an all-sky optical survey system featuring a 6-foot (1.8 m) telescope being set up at the Oak Ridge Observatory in Massachusetts, are underway to further advance optical SETI development.

## Turn up the radio

In the 1960s, Frank Drake argued that the way to find far-off civilizations was through radio. Radio waves travel at the speed of light, so it would make sense that alien civilizations would use such a signal to test for life before making the long journey to Earth to investigate. Drake joined the National Radio Astronomy Observatory, where he "listened" to radio transmissions that were given off by galaxies, stars, and even cosmic dust, in search of some indication of deliberate transmissions. He and his colleagues devised a plan to increase their odds of locating intelligent life. They targeted those frequencies emitted by hydrogen, the oxygen-hydrogen molecule, and the water molecule, because water is life's most basic need and hydrogen is the most abundant element. Drake and his crew spent hundreds of hours collecting and evaluating signals in search of organized patterns. His patterns of ones and zeros contained a hidden meaning that these targeted alien civilizations would have to have the inclination and the ability to decipher. As well, it would take a long time to send and then receive a message, but it was something Drake was willing and eager to undertake.

As technology advanced, more sophisticated equipment could do in seconds what Drake had toiled over for weeks. Today, the National Radio Astronomy Observatory (NRAO), set up with funding from the U.S. government, provides cutting-edge radio-telescope facilities to further scientific discovery. This not-for-profit organization designs, builds, and operates these telescopes in order for scientists from around the world to study everything from planets in our solar system to the unknown possibilities at the fringes of space. These telescopes can monitor signals in space to determine if other

## STARS MOST LIKELY TO HARBOR LIFE

In early 2006, a U.S. astronomer at the Carnegie Institution in Washington, D.C., announced a shortlist of the stars most likely to harbor intelligent life. Margaret Turnbull looked at criteria such as the star's age and the amount of iron in its atmosphere. Her top five picks were:

- **Beta CVn:** A sun-like star 26 light-years away in the constellation Canes Venatici (the hound dogs)
- **HD 10307:** Has almost the same mass, temperature, and iron content as the sun
- **HD 211 415:** Has about half the metal content of the sun and is a bit cooler
- **18 Sco:** A near match for the sun in the constellation Scorpio
- **51 Pegasus:** A Jupiter-like planet has been found here; may also host planets like Earth.

civilizations are contacting Earth, or any other civilization, for that matter.

Project Phoenix was the most comprehensive search for extraterrestrial intelligence in the world to date and used the largest radio telescope in the southern hemisphere—located in New South Wales, Australia. It followed NASA's

1992 Microwave Observing Program (MOP) funded by the U.S. government. It was a specific, targeted search of 800 nearby stars, as well as a sweep of the sky in general. This program was to provide long-term research into SETI, using various radio dishes that would carefully analyze the data. However, U.S. Congress ridiculed the program and MOP was cancelled after only one year. But SETI supporters took the foundation created by MOP and created Project Phoenix. This 1995 project, led by the former-NASA project scientist Dr. Jill Tarter, involved listening to radio signals to detect messages that might be sent intentionally to Earth by other faraway civilizations. The search also used the Green Bank telescope in West Virginia between 1996 and 1998. Project Phoenix targeted about 1000 nearby, sun-like stars (all within about 200 light-years), which were most likely to host planets capable of life. While this project does not require a scientist with headphones, astronomers evaluate those signals picked up

## RADIO TELESCOPES

There are some impressive radio telescopes at the disposal of researchers today. The **Very Large Array** (VLA) in New Mexico is one of the world's best astronomical radio observatories. There, 27 82-foot (25 m) diameter radio antennas collect data from great distances away.

The **Green Bank telescope** in West Virginia is about 330 feet (100 m) across and offers scientists a view of the entire sky above five degrees elevation with precise pointing. It is the largest fully mobile radio telescope in the world. It is in an area made free of electromagnetic pollution to aid in signal reception.

The **Very Long Baseline Array** (VLBA) is the largest full-time astronomical telescope in the world. It's a series of 10 telescopes with 82-foot (25 m) diameter dishes. These telescopes span more than 5000 miles (8050 km), giving astronomers the best and sharpest vision of any telescope.

The **Arecibo radio telescope** is an enormous telescope, measuring 1000 feet (305 m) across, 167 feet (51 m) deep, and stands on about 20 acres. It is the world's most sensitive telescope, picking up the faintest signals from the farthest corners of the cosmos.

by the computer that are unusual or interesting in some way. This project made it possible to detect power output from transmitters about 200 light-years away. By the middle of 1999, Project Phoenix had investigated about half of the stars it planned to target. By 2004, the project had scanned 800 stars on its list. To that point, there had been no discernible, extraterrestrial message received.

But that message may be only a day away, and the future welcomes a new telescope created exclusively for the search for extraterrestrial intelligence 24 hours a day, seven days a week. The Allen Telescope Array, funded by Microsoft co-founder Paul Allen and former Microsoft chief technology officer Nathan Myhrvold, will include an array of 350 antennas at the Hat Creek Observatory in northern California. It will allow researchers to scan many different targets at the same time. Given the number of 19.7-foot (6 m) diameter dishes, this facility will boast a collection area greater than that of a 328-foot (100 m) telescope. For the first time, SETI will have the capacity to thoroughly examine a large sample of space—an enormous leap forward for SETI research. Project construction began in November 2005 with 42 dishes and will continue with three more phases: 56 more dishes by July 2006, 108 more slated for April 2007, and the final 144 dishes completed by June 2008. When it is finished, the Allen Telescope Array will be one of the world's largest and most powerful telescopes.

## The king debunker

Although Philip Klass was an electrical engineer and aviation specialist, most people knew him as the man who discredited UFO and alien visitation claims. He believed that most "UFO activity" could easily explained away as balloons, kites, meteors, and the like. Klass argued that physical marks, such as scars, that "victims" could not remember getting, were often from forgotten childhood injuries. He also found explanations for circles on the ground, missing time, and other common indicators of alien visitation. While Klass didn't believe aliens were landing on Earth, he was open and eager to be proven wrong—even inviting alien abduction, so that he could stop working so hard to validate (and consequently debunk) such claims. He went so far as to offer $10,000 to anyone who reported an alien abduction to the FBI that was backed up by that agency. That reward was never collected.

Klass insisted that he was not out to disprove the existence of UFOs and alien visitation, but rather was dedicated to finding the truth. It so happened that the truth Klass found supported prosaic explanations for alleged sightings or showed fabricated stories of abductions and encounters. In an interview with the television show *NOVA*, Klass said:

> *There is simply no scientifically credible evidence that we have alien visitors. If there were, there would no longer be a mystery; there would no longer*

*be a controversy ... So even if the idea of extraterrestrial visitors is a bit far out, we've had more than 50 years to come up with artifacts, with evidence. And nobody has been able to come up with it.*

Klass was first drawn into the world of ufology in 1966, when he was a senior editor of *Aviation Week & Space Technology*—a magazine that ran articles on space technology and travel, making Klass somewhat of an expert. A police officer in New Mexico claimed he saw aliens climbing into a spacecraft and zipping away. Klass determined that the claim was a hoax concocted by the Socorro native in order to drum up more tourism for the area. Klass became involved in countless other cases of alien encounters and researched the Roswell UFO claims in great detail for several years. He wrote many books and articles on the subject, plus a newsletter called *Skeptics UFO Newsletter*.

While many people found him to be a thorough scientist, he had staunch critics that felt his methods were aggressive and closed-minded, and accused the skeptic of "dirty tricks" to discredit stories of UFO sightings. Others claimed he misrepresented facts in order to support his explanation of events.

Klass was one of the founding members of the Committee for the Scientific Investigation of Claims of the Paranormal (CSICOP), which studies claims for scientific validity. This organization boasts a wide network of people across the United States that conducts research and analyzes fringe events for scientific bases. Other recognizable names on CSICOP's, membership list have included television science host Bill Nye and the late Carl Sagan and Isaac Asimov. Members doggedly scrutinize every claim of paranormal activity. They believe that if a claim cannot be proven scientifically, it is baseless. This approach fits perfectly with Klass's passion for science and scientific methods. He continued his study and maintained a keen interest in ufology until his death in August 2005.

## Center for UFO Studies (CUFOS)

In the 1950s and 1960s, Dr. J. Allen Hynek was a professor of astronomy at Ohio State University and chairman of the astronomy department at Northwestern University. This scientist was also a consultant for the United States Air Force's Project Blue Book. It was his job to establish any possible astronomical reason—such as a meteor or Venus visible—which could explain a UFO sighting. Dr. Hynek was critical of alien encounters and UFOs when he began, but over time as he studied case after case, he decided that the UFO phenomenon deserved serious consideration.

At a symposium on the topic in 1968, Dr. Hynek said that the UFO problem "has been made immensely more difficult by the supposition held by most scientists, on the basis of the poor data available to them, that there couldn't possibly be anything substantial to UFO reports in the first place, and hence that there is no point to wasting time or money investigating." To help turn this misconception around, he established the Center for UFO Studies in 1973. This organization consisted of scientists and specialists who, together, would tackle the mystery of UFOs. Dr. Hynek remained active in CUFOS until his death in 1986.

Today, CUFOS is an international organization of volunteers, investigators, and academics who analyze UFO reports. It also keeps an archive and library of everything to do with UFOs, from books to sighting reports. CUFOS publishes a magazine called the *International UFO Reporter* as well as a scholarly edition called the *Journal of UFO Studies*. In addition, the center investigates fascinating areas surrounding ufology. For example, some CUFOS investigators are delving into the Roswell incident, while others are preparing a psychological profile of people claiming to have been abducted by aliens. Finally, the Center for UFO Studies responds to sightings and studies reports from around the world to determine their credibility.

## Dr. John Mack

One wouldn't expect a Pulitzer Prize winning author and Harvard Medical School psychiatry professor to become fascinated by UFOs and alien encounters. However, Dr. John Mack did just that. He was intrigued by how our perceptions affect our relationships with others and with the world around us. This led him to the study of alien encounters and especially abductions—a phenomenon to which he had not given much credence before. As he learned more about it and spoke to more people claiming to have been abducted, Dr. Mack was impressed by the consistencies in the stories (even across geographic expanses) and the power of the emotion attached to these experiences. As well, many of the abduction claims coincided with independent reports of strange sightings in the areas involved.

Dr. Mack had to change his worldview and way of thinking while working in this area. In an interview on *NOVA*, Dr. Mack said: "The phenomenon stretches us, or it asks us to stretch to open to realities that are not simply the literal physical world, but to extend to the possibilities that there are other unseen realities from which our consciousness, our, if you will, learning processes, over the past several hundred years have closed us off." He opened himself up and gave the study of ufology a new face that was backed by impressive professional credentials.

In 1992, Dr. Mack co-chaired the Scientific Assembly on Alien Encounters Abduction Study Conference held at the prestigious Massachusetts Institute of Technology, and the following year, he created the Program for Extraordinary Experience Research (PEER) to frame his studies in this area. Through this organization, Dr. Mack and his team spoke with more than 200 people from six continents about their experiences with unknown life forms. He offered them support and counseling to deal with the trauma of their encounters, even arranging group support meetings in his home.

For Dr. Mack, alien abduction was a topic of scientific and clinical interest. He looked at it as a way to learn more about the human psyche and to expand our definitions of psychological and physical realities. He acknowledged the controversial nature of his study—becoming accustomed and unfazed by the disrespect and ridicule heaped on him because of it—but argued that the effect of the UFO encounter or alien abduction on the "victim" and treating that person was all that mattered.

Dr. Mack reluctantly began to believe in those who reported alien encounters or abductions, and spent the latter part of his life working intensively with "experiencers" to study it further. While he didn't publicly comment on what he thought was the literal truth of abduction cases or if the events were "real," he did contend that the experiences are real for experiencers and that these people should be respected rather than written off as mentally ill or troublemakers.

During his career, Dr. John Mack wrote or co-wrote 11 books, including, *Abduction: Human Encounters with Aliens* in 1994 and *Passport to the Cosmos: Human Transformation and Alien Encounters* in 1999. He also wrote more than 150 scholarly articles. Dr. Mack was struck and killed by a drunk driver in 2004, while crossing the street after participating in a T.E. Lawrence symposium in England. The John E. Mack Institute continues his studies in various areas of the human experience.

# CHAPTER 5

# The Future

A stronomer Frank Drake created an equation to estimate the number of intelligent civilizations that might exist in the universe. With that number in the millions, it would seem that the search for such life should be a priority. However, other scientists, including the University of Washington's Peter Ward and Donald Brownlee, have put forth their rare-Earth hypothesis, which states that Earth is unique, so life replicated elsewhere is unlikely. They contend that a number of factors came together to make life on Earth possible—living in the habitable area of the sun, having a planet like Jupiter to clear away space debris, and having few mass extinctions. They say that these factors are specific to Earth, explaining why life developed here, but nowhere else.

## Is there anybody out there?

If the answer is yes, modern science is making great strides to find it. Scientists from across the continent are part of a North American initiative to see more deeply into space. Great minds from across Canada and the United States are coming together at the California Institute of Technology headquarters to create the world's largest telescope as part of the Thirty Meter Telescope (TMT) project. While the telescope won't be fully operational for another 10 to 15 years, it promises to be well worth the wait. It is expected to make the Hubble telescope seem almost like a magnifying glass: the new telescope will have 100 times more power than Hubble. This will open the skies and allow scientists to view 10 billion light-years into space. The possibilities that this telescope present are exciting and may lead to insights into the debate over alien life in space.

Ufologists and believers are optimistic that the age-old question of whether there are civilizations beyond our knowledge will soon be answered. It is a question posed by many great minds, including physicist Enrico Fermi, who spent a great deal of time pondering the existence of technologically advanced civilization in the universe. The Fermi Paradox asks where such civilizations are, and if there are many advanced alien civilizations, why has evidence of this existence eluded people on Earth for centuries? The paradox suggests that the two contentions are oppositional—if there are so many civilizations, there should be some signs, such as probes or radio transmissions. So, Fermi states, either intelligent life is, in fact, rare and our current observations are incomplete, and so we haven't yet received these signs, or the way in which we are searching for them is faulty. Increased SETI research across the world is aiming to resolve this paradox, and scientists and enthusiasts alike are optimistic that revelations are just around the corner.

# A Timeline of Alien Encounters

**1947**   Kenneth Arnold reports first wave of U.S. "flying disk" sightings in Washington, thus launching the modern UFO era.

Rumors of a flying disk and occupants recovered near Roswell, New Mexico.

Project Blue Book established.

**1948**   Project Sign is the first long-term official UFO investigation tool conducted by air force.

Captain Thomas Mantell becomes first known casualty of the UFO phenomenon.

**1949**   Donald Keyhoe publishes an article in *True Magazine*, becoming the first to assert in a major publication that UFOs are alien craft and that the

government is withholding information from the public.

**1950**    Paul Trent photographs hovering UFO

**1951**    An incredible 1,501 reports of UFO sightings logged

**1952**    Project Blue Book launched to study UFO phenomenon

Aerial Phenomenon Research Organization becomes first long-term UFO association

Major wave of sightings leading to air force admitting that they are unexplained

George Adamski claims he communicated with an alien being from Venus using mental telepathy and hand signals.

**1953**    CIA-sponsored panel of scientists states that UFO sightings are likely mistakes

Adamski goes public with story of contact with alien life forms

**1956** Bentwaters Air Force Base in Great Britain experiences strange sightings for five hours, witnessed from the air, ground, and on radar.

**1957** Brazil's Antonio Villas Boas becomes the first recorded alien abductee.

**1964** UFO reported to have landed with crew near Socorro, New Mexico, and policeman becomes first "Close Encounter of the Third Kind." This case was also the only one to be considered "unexplained" by Project Blue Book.

**1967** Wesleyan University becomes the first to offer credit courses on UFOs.

**1969** The University of Colorado's UFO study, also known as the Condon Report, releases a

controversial summary that UFO enthusiasts say is not representative of the positive portions of the report.

**1969** Project Blue Book is canceled.

Walter Andrus establishes Mutual UFO Network (MUFON).

Astronauts land on the moon and there are rumors that they were not alone.

**1974** Astronomer Frank Drake sends the first deliberate communication from Earth targeting extraterrestrials, using the Arecibo Observatory in Puerto Rico.

**1975** Travis Walton is reportedly abducted for five days.

**1984** The SETI Institute is founded.

**1987** Public interest in alien abductions fueled by release of bestselling books.

Alleged MJ-12 report details recovery of alien spacecraft at Roswell in 1947, but this remains controversial.

**1989** Linda Napolitano claims aliens abducted her from her bedroom in New York City.

**1990** The Center for the Study of Extraterrestrial Intelligence is established.

**1991** Roper Organization poll claims that as many as four million Americans could be alien abductees.

**1992** MUFON, CUFOS, and Fund for UFO Research come together to create the UFO Research Coalition in order to better manage joint problems.

**1995** Alien autopsy film released allegedly showing examination of a crash victim from Roswell in 1947.

**1995**    Project Phoenix is launched using the largest radio telescope to monitor radio signals in search of otherworldly messages.

**1997**    The Phoenix Lights UFO sighting case draws thousands of witnesses across the country.

**2005**    Construction begins on the Allen Telescope Array, which will be the largest and most powerful in the world.

NASA launches a Mars Reconnaissance Orbiter (MRO) to search for life in space.

**2006**    On March 11, the MRO successfully parked itself in an elliptical orbit around the Red Planet.

# Amazing Facts and Figures

- In 1964, Canada built the world's first UFO landing pad, which is in St. Paul, Alberta.

- In December 2005, a Taiwan-based company donated $20 million to build a UFO research facility in China.

### Unexplained phenomena

- In 1917, 50,000 people in Fatima, Portugal, reported seeing an enormous spinning disk come out of the clouds. Many claimed it gave off such heat that their clothes, wet from rain, were dry in minutes. The disk dropped toward Earth and then soared back into the sky and disappeared.

- During World War II, Allied pilots reported seeing odd balls of light beside their airplanes. They dubbed them "foo fighters" and believed they were secret weapons or surveillance devices created by the Germans. But German pilots reported seeing the same glowing balls. Some researchers claim these balls of light were actually UFOs.

- There were other incidents similar to Roswell that renewed interest in the mystery of the 1947 crash site. The Keeksburg UFO incident in Pennsylvania in 1965 and the Rendlesham Forest incident in the United Kingdom in 1980 both got people thinking about the "real" story behind those strange events in New Mexico.

- In 1949, an elliptical object that military engineers calculated was traveling at around 18,000 miles (29,000 km) per hour was sighted over White Sands Proving Grounds in New Mexico. Commander Robert McLaughlin reported that he was sure that what he saw was "a flying saucer, and further, that these disks are spaceships from another planet."

- When Ronald Reagan was a governor in 1972, he spoke about his own UFO encounter. He claimed to have seen a bright white light out of the window of an airplane. He asked the pilot to follow it, which he did for several minutes until the light shot into the sky above the plane.

- In 1972, the United States sent a plaque inscribed with a cryptic message into space attached to the antenna support struts of a space probe. Another message meant for alien civilizations was dispatched the same way the following year. In 1980, another probe contained a recording of an earthly greeting spoken in 54 languages.

• There are areas that experience a larger number of sightings than any others. One such location is around the Yakima Indian Reservation in Washington State. Some ufologists claim that the region is a "window" for spacecraft. Between 1964 and 1984, there were 186 reported sightings on the reservation.

• Astronauts allegedly use the code name "Santa Claus" to refer to alien spacecraft when on missions. There have been a few instances in which astronauts have stated: "There is a Santa Claus."

• Between 2001 and 2002, UFO sightings in Canada rose by 42 percent. Of those, 15 percent remained unexplained and the rest were either explainable or investigators lacked the necessary information to assess the report. There were 39 percent more sightings in 2003 than in 2002, with 17 percent unexplained. (Source: *Canadian UFO Survey*)

## Crop circles
• About 10,000 crop circles have been reported around the world to date.

- While crop circles have appeared in 70 countries around the world, they seem to be heavily concentrated in southern England, around such ancient sites as Stonehenge, Avebury, and Silbury Hill.

- The longest crop circle formed was in Wiltshire, England in 1996. This chain of circles and adjoining pathways was 4100 feet (1.2 km) long and stretched from one end of the field to the other.

## Opinion polls

- In June 1997 in the United Kingdom, the largest opinion poll on the topic of UFOs was conducted after a live television debate called "Strange but True." About seven million people responded to the question: "Have aliens already visited Earth?" Ninety-two percent answered yes. Three days later, the television station followed up with a telephone poll and asked respondents if they believed aliens exist. Of the 2215 people contacted, 87 percent answered "yes."

- A poll in 1997 revealed that about three million Canadians have witnessed some form of UFO encounter. It also showed that:
    - 78 percent of Canadians believe that life exists elsewhere in the universe.
    - More than 52 percent believe that some

UFOs are alien spacecraft.
- Only 12 percent of people actually report UFO sightings.
- More than 57 percent of Canadians believe there is a military or government cover-up regarding the existence of UFOs.

• A January 2000 nationwide poll by Yankelovich Partners revealed that one percent of American adults believe that they have encountered beings from other planets.

• A Gallup Poll in May 2000 revealed that 33 percent of Americans believe that extraterrestrial beings have visited Earth, while another 27 percent aren't sure they haven't.

• A Roper Poll conducted for the Sci-Fi Channel in 2002 found that about 75 percent of Americans believe extraterrestrial life is out there and will be discovered. More than half of people polled expressed an interest in personally encountering alien life on Earth. It also stated that 48 percent of respondents believed that alien UFOs have visited Earth.

## Science and research
• The Aerial Phenomena Research Organization was a research group devoted to UFO study

between 1952 and 1988. Founders Jim and Coral Lorenzen emphasized scientific field investigations with the assistance of a staff of PhD scientists. One such reputable scientist was the University of Arizona's Dr. James E. McDonald, an atmospheric physicist and one of the best scientific UFO researchers of the time.

- Since SETI@home launched in 1999, it has logged more than two million years of combined computing time. By the end of September 2001, the program had completed 1021 operations, earning it a place in the *Guinness Book of World Records* as the largest computation.

- The Allen Telescope Array will be able to study many areas simultaneously. This offers an incredible advantage over other projects (including Project Phoenix's stellar reconnaissance of 1000 stars) with the ability to study 100,000 or even one million nearby stars.

- More than 90 percent of reported UFOs can be scientifically explained. But not all UFO sightings involve witnesses perpetrating a hoax. In fact, less than one percent of reported encounters are deliberate hoaxes.

# What Others Say

"If I become President, I'll make every piece of information this country has about UFO sightings available to the public and the scientists … I am convinced UFOs exist because I have seen one."

*Jimmy Carter during the 1976 presidential election campaign*

"Personally, I think it can be safely said that the visitation of this planet by extraterrestrial intelligences is now a confirmed fact."

*Alan Watts, author*

"I am quite confident that there is no scientific credible evidence to show that we've had alien visitors, let alone that they're doing these dreadful things."

*Philip Klass, UFO researcher*

"You have the sense that these people have actually experienced something of great meaning and depth and profundity that is not simply a projection of their own unconscious."

*Dr. John Mack, Pulitzer Prize winning author*

"I'm convinced beyond doubt that we have recovered aircraft, alien vehicles, that we have made contact with aliens, that we are communicating with them in some way or form, and that we have vehicles and bodies in preservation."

*Lt. Col. Wendele Stevens, former foreign technology division officer*

"Make no mistake, Roswell happened. I've seen secret files which show the government knew about it—but decided not to tell the public."

*Dr. Edgar Mitchell,*
*Project Apollo astronaut*

"The U.S. military are preparing weapons which could be used against the aliens, and they could get us into an intergalactic war ... The Bush administration has finally agreed to let the military build a forward base on the moon, which will put them in a better position to keep track of the goings and comings of the visitors from space, and to shoot at them, if they so decide."

*Paul Hellyer, former Canadian*
*defense minister and deputy*
*prime minister in the 1960s*

"Can we afford not to look toward UFO skies; can we afford to overlook a potential breakthrough of great significance? And even apart from that, the public is growing impatient. The public does not want another 20 years of UFO confusion..."

*Dr. Allen Hynek at a 1968 symposium on UFOs*

"Their bald heads were disproportionately large for their puny bodies. They had bulging, oversized craniums, a small jaw structure, and an underdeveloped appearance to their features that was almost infantile."

*Travis Walton, about the aliens that abducted him*

"NASA has developed a high-tech sanitizing protocol to bounce transmissions from the astronauts off a number lof satellites so as to prevent private parties on Earth from receiving uncensored messages."

*William J. Birnes in his book "The UFO Magazine UFO Encyclopedia" on NASA's attempt to hide the truth about UFOs*

"We didn't know where it came from. It happened too fast. Its lights turned from bright reddish orange to a whitish blue … Green lights rotated round the edge of the saucer. A little girl or woman wearing a white night gown sailed out of the window in a fetal position—and then stood in mid-air in this beam of light. I could see three of the ugliest creatures I ever saw. I don't know what they were. They weren't human."

*"Richard," alleged government agent on witnessing Linda Napolitano's abduction*

"The evidence that the Earth is being visited by at least one extraterrestrial civilization is extensive both in scope and detail. In its totality, it comprises a body of evidence which at the very least supports the general assessment that extraterrestrial life has been detected, and that a vigorous program of research and serious diplomatic initiatives is warranted."

*Dr. Steven Greer, director of the Center for the Study of Extra-Terrestrial Intelligence*

# Photo Credits

Cover: Getty Images/Antonio M. Rosario; page 8: AP Photo; page 9: AP Photo/Mississippi Press; page 10: AP Photo/Air Force; page 11: AP Photo/John Todd; page 12: James Aylott/Getty Images; page 13: AP Photo/Detroit Free Press, Susan Tusa.